CONCILIUM

Religion in the Eighties

CONCILIUM

General Secretariat: Prins Bernhardstraat 2, 6521 AB Nijmegen, The Netherlands

Concilium 206 (6/1989): Feminist Theology

CONCILIUM

List of Members

Advisory Commitee: Feminist Theology

MOTHERHOOD: EXPERIENCE, INSTITUTION, THEOLOGY

Edited by
Anne Carr
and
Elisabeth Schüssler Fiorenza

English Language Editor
Philip Hillyer

T & T CLARK
Edinburgh

December 1989
ISBN: 0 567 30086 2

ISSN: 0010-5236

Typeset by C. R. Barber & Partners (Highlands) Ltd, Fort William
Printed by Page Brothers (Norwich) Ltd

Concilium: Published February, April, June, August, October, December.
Subscriptions 1989: UK: £29.95 (including postage and packing); USA: US$49.95 (including air mail postage and packing); Canada: Canadian$64.95 (including air mail postage and packing); other countries: £29.95 (including postage and packing).

Contents

CONCILIUM 206 Special Column

Mary-John Mananzan

The Cost of Commitment: The Persecution of Christians in Southeast Asia

AS THE body of Fred Veraguas, an assassinated Church lay worker of Kimamaymaya Parish in Mindanao, Philippines, was lowered into the grave, the Church people mourning him chanted, 'Mabuhay ang Bago-ong Martir sang Kristianong Katilingban'. (Long live the new martyr of the Christian Community.) And they recalled the names of other new Christian martyrs who have given up their lives—Fr Favali, Fr Rudy Romano, Fr Alberto Romero, Pastor Amado Anosa, Fr Mario Estorba, Fr Dionisio Malalay, Rev Vizminda Gran and her husband Lovello, Liza Obrero, Sr Vivian Doromal, etc., etc.; 120 victims in three years!

The PCPR (Promotion of Church People's Reports) gives a breakdown of the documented cases of human rights violations of Church people between February 1986–May 1989:

Of the 132 cases of human rights violations, 352 Church people were reported victims. 120 or 34.09 per cent were killed, 72 or 20.45 per cent were falsely charged by the court; 13 or 3.69 per cent were either falsely accused of being communist or communist sympathisers; 30 or 8.52 per cent were arrested; 31 or 8.81 per cent were survivors of frustrated murder; 46 or 13.17 per cent were victims of grenade throwings, bombings or arsons; 26 or 7.39 per cent were harassed. Also, there were two reported victims of torture and another two of abduction. Six victims were arrested and detained, three were illegally searched and one abducted and detained. (From PCPR Update, p. 2.)

These relentless killings and harassment confirm a pattern of persecution of progressive elements in the Church in the Philippines. On the occasion of the killing of Fr Dionisio Malalay and Mr Rufino Rivera on 2 April 1989 the Bishop and clergy and people of the Diocese of Pagadian wrote a statement of protest which declared:

> *Since 1987 we have grieved at the loss of nine Church leaders from the diocese who have been brutally killed by government forces (four others had already been killed during the Marcos regime). Combine this high rate of killing of Church personnel with the constant harassment of Church people through blatant attempts of intimidation by propaganda, lies and threats to their very lives and it becomes relatively clear why we consider ourselves to be living in a period of Church persecution in the Philippines. It is not an exaggeration to say that practically all efforts of Church people to promote life, even such attempts as organising the people for health, farming for reforestation, for liturgical celebration and Bible sharings, for protection and promotion of Tribal communities, are labelled as communist activities. To the outsider this may seem a harmless enough accusation, but to the people being accused, it is a life and death issue because anyone who is associated with such activities is considered by the military to be communist and therefore can be summarily executed by military forces . . . (From the Statement of the Pagadian Church People on the Brutal Killing of Fr Dionisio Malalay and Mr Rufino Rivera, 12 August 1989.)*

Such witch-hunting and persecution of progressive Church people is not confined to the Philippines.

There is the case of the Singapore Sixteen. These sixteen people, among them four full-time Church workers and six Church volunteers were arrested on 2 May and 22 June 1987 by the Internal Security Department in an operation codenamed 'Spectrum'. They were charged with being involved in a 'marxist plot to overthrow the government'. The key figure among the sixteen is Vincent Cheng, full-time secretary of the Singapore Archdiocesan Justice and Peace Commission who was made to appear on TV in a 'confession' interview. Although the Archbishop initially issued a statement that prayed for the detainees, after the so-called 'confession' he accepted the evidence against Cheng. He also suspended four priests who resigned from their posts to show their dissatisfaction with the acceptance of the government's accusation. He also ordered other priests 'not to mix religion and politics in their sermons'.

Some months later, the Christian Conference of Asia was expelled from Singapore for championing the cause of the accused. In February 1989 the National Council of Churches of Singapore withdrew its membership from the CCA.

Five months later, on 27 October 1987, a similar crackdown took place in Malaysia resulting in the mass detention of progressive personalities, including Church people.

These growing incidents of the persecution of Church people in Southeast Asia which also occur in other places in the Third World ranging from negative propaganda, harassment, false accusation, arbitrary arrests, detention torture, kidnapping and even assassination and massacre invite us to reflect on the cost of living one's Christian commitment in today's world.

When one analyses all these cases of persecution of Church people, one thing stands out as common to many of them. They all lived their faith and preached the good news of integral salvation within the Church's declared preferential option for the poor and the oppressed and in solidarity with the struggling and suffering people of God. These are people who have begun to understand the social dimension of their faith. They have realised that salvation is not the 'salvation of the soul, from sin, hell and death, in order to go to heaven' but means the total and concrete salvation of the human person, body and soul not only individually but in the context of a social milieu. This holistic understanding of salvation urges them to struggle against the obstacles to an integral total human liberation which they discover to be imbedded in economic, political and social structures. This leads them to make a consequent option for the oppressed, which of course has political consequences that draw the ire of the rich and powerful who benefit from the oppressive system and exploit and oppress the great majority of the people. Depending upon the threat they pose to the powers that be, Church people become the target of retaliation or elimination by those whose interests are threatened by their commitment.

These incidents should evoke righteous indignation from all decent people, even if more often than not the hierarchy seems to be blind and deaf to their plight. Bishops, easily taken in by the 'red scare', readily acquiesce in the accusations of civil authorities and to the blackmail of the military who conveniently provide them with evidences of 'moral lapses' of the accused especially if they are priests or religious. These people are marginalised in the Church because their ideas and activities disturb, and their questionings threaten the more traditional elements which are, of course, the majority. And yet they are the ones that are actually seeing to it that the truest, the noblest, and the most authentic in the Church and Christianity will go on. And it is actually the 'loyalists' in the Church who in their intransigent clinging to the past are in fact digging the grave for an obsolete Church. But prophets are never recognised by their own people. Every generation kills its prophets. Prophecy and martyrdom go together and these guarantee the continuous rebirth of the Church. A biblico-theological reflection entitled 'God is at work in the people's struggles' concludes thus:

> *Being part of the people, the emerging Church also shares with the suffering of the people. Those who belong to this Church have the marks of the crucified (John 20:26–29). Some of them are arrested, tortured, involuntary disappeared, or summarily executed. Nevertheless they remain faithful to the God who is at work in the struggle of the people, like the Lamb slain yet standing to give hope and life to the victims of the 'feast'. (Rev. 5)*

Truly these modern martyrs are the source of our hope and inspiration.

Note that this Special Column, like others in this series, is written under the sole responsibility of the author.

MOTHERHOOD: EXPERIENCE, INSTITUTION, THEOLOGY

Editorial

IN THIS number of *Concilium*, we explore motherhood as a theological concept in the light of Adrienne Rich's important distinction between the potential relationship of every woman to her powers of reproduction and to children on the one hand, and motherhood as a social, cultural, and religious institution and ideology on the other. It is the institution of motherhood that keeps this potential, and women and children, under patriarchal control, and disempowers women. This distinction between experience and institution provides the basis for feminist analysis of motherhood as a source for theological reflection.

Our intention in dealing with the theme of motherhood as experience, institution and theology is to expose some of the ways in which patriarchal sexism has shaped cultural, religious and Christian understandings of women and to indicate some of the critical perspectives which feminist theory affords today. It is our hope that in the light of these perspectives on the differences, indeed contradictions, between experience and institution that a critical feminist theological reflection on motherhood might be developed.

Ursula Pfäfflin opens our first section with an analysis of motherhood in feminist experience and theory. She examines psychological, psychoanalytical, and sociological theories about the different development of girls and boys in 'mother-dominated' nuclear families and raises the question of whether the 'mystique of motherhood' differs among different classes, races and cultures. Pfäfflin's overview surveys some of the most important developments in recent feminist practice and theory and sketches implications for a post-patriarchal culture, politics, philosophy, and spirituality. She argues that a new paradigm of motherhood has the capacity not only for overcoming the split between the worlds of women and men but also splits among different cultures, nations, races, classes, and religions. In tracing the outlines of a new spirituality of motherhood, she suggests the power of mothers for both material and spiritual transformation.

In our next essay, Mercy Oduyoye reflects on poverty and motherhood from a Third World perspective that highlights the interconnections and disparities that show why the majority of the poor in the world are women and their children. She uses her particular African experience and social location to analyse the androcentrism of the systems of global patriarchy, its effects on women and children, and the strategies of survival that have marked the experience of African mothers. In pointing to the political and economic causes of poverty, she argues for the empowerment of women in the management of creation, the earth, the human community, and the nation as the home of women and men, rich and poor, concluding that the survival of humankind is the responsibility of both women and men.

In a different cultural context, Marie-Thérèse van Lunen Chenu highlights some of the contradictions between women's lived experiences and institutional Church teachings on women and motherhood. She relates her personal experience as an ordinary Catholic mother in the West, and the experience of her grown children, to the recent papal letter on the dignity of women as she describes the feminist search for the buried word of revelation in the patriarchal order of the Church. She sees the limitations of the letter in its affirmation that motherhood is not merely a possible but an essential vocation of women, validated by the archetype of Mary, while Jesus is the archetype for men. She argues that the nuptial symbolism, with its maternal and spousal imagery, so dominates the theology of the Church in this letter that one searches in vain for the symbols of Christian renewal—people, body, community. The letter's theological construction of the Church as mother not only fails to relate to the experience of women in the Church today but reproduces the asymmetric gender-dualism of Western culture.

The final essay in our opening section on experience and institution approaches the Catholic tradition of spiritual motherhood, particularly as it is embodied in the institution of the Mother Superior in canonical communities. Ivone Gebara indicates the experiential bases for the tradition and its iconoclastic transformations in the context of Latin American liberation movements. She shows how the poor in Latin America challenge the escapist, other-worldly spirituality of the hierarchical and patriarchal model of the Church. In Latin America, it is the popular leaders, both women and men, who are retrieving the original intuition of spiritual motherhood in a new way. Their dream of a new reality for their nations is expressed in poetry, sermon, and liturgy for the spiritual nourishment of the people.

In our second section on the ethics and politics of motherhood, Christine Gudorf broadens the basis of reflection and sketches the beginnings of a cross-cultural analysis of women's choices. She explores three issues: women's choice about marriage, choice about sexual intercourse in or outside marriage, and social coercion with respect to birth control and child care. She compares statistics for nations of the Middle East, the Soviet Union, African and Latin American countries, China, India, Bangladesh, the United States and other developed nations in terms of cultural, legal and religions traditions, as well as offering class analysis. Her discussion reveals some appalling accounts: genital mutilation of women and forced contraceptive programmes in Africa, wife-beating and men's abandonment of women and children in Latin America, coerced contraception, abortion, and infanticide (especially of female babies) in China, the sexual availability of a wife to her husband or his brothers, the killing of wives for dowry, and the coerced sterilisation of the poor in India and Bangladesh. She points out the economic, political, and medical contexts of women's lack of choice in situations where mothers are expected to provide child care and do household work in addition to work outside the home; women in most countries average nearly double the hours of work that men contribute. Gudorf urges as minimum criteria for a responsible ethic of motherhood: respect for women's rights to make decisions about marriage, sex, work, contraception; opening of alternative female roles, including but not requiring motherhood and child care; respect for women and their bodies and for sexual interaction as mutuality, not domination; acceptance by men of equal responsibility for child care, housework, and financial support for children; social support of parenting in paid maternity leave and affordable, quality child care; non-coercive access for all women to safe contraception; social support for lowering maternal and infant mortality rates by addressing poverty, which afflicts women and children most.

Johanna Kohn-Roelin explores the complex psychological, sociological and theological dimensions of the socialisation of women to motherhood, pointing to the contradiction between the social and ecclesiastical acknowledgment of the value of motherhood and the social and ecclesiastical position of real mothers. She shows that the idealisation of the mother, a nineteenth-century phenomenon, meant the privatisation of love and religion in the private realm of the family where the woman reigned in a kind of 'powerless power' while the father vanished from family life. His absence meant the social reduction of the family, where the mother prepared the children for rigid sex-specific roles. Girls found their model for the future in the mother, a role confirmed by society and Church as it is in the recent papal letter on women, where women are called to the loving service of real or spiritual motherhood but not ordination to official service in the Church. The middle-class religious ideal of motherhood simply excludes employed married women, and lesbian or single women who balance motherhood and work outside the home. Feminist theology, Kohn-Roelin argues, concerns *all* women, whether they are mothers or not, because each woman is the daughter of a mother. She sketches the theory of N. Chodorow on the psychological reproduction of motherhood and offers some suggestions about the problem of dependence and autonomy for the feminist daughter. And she urges the development of new roles of mother and father, indicating the relation between the image of God and children's early experience of parents and of the Church.

Dorry de Beijer examines the new reproductive technologies in the light of patriarchal ideology and institutions, and feminist questions about women's choice. Test-tube babies, surrogate motherhood, genetic planning and infertility clinics are the result of reproductive research that is often bases on a framework of father-right that ignores women's bodily integrity: motherhood can be reduced to the notion of passive breeding ground in the ideology of patriarchal control. While the new technologies can be liberating for women in providing the possibility of children, it is essential that they be seen in the context of women's right to choose. A new perspective is called for that integrates relationality, physicality, and creativity in an authentic ethic of respect for women and their continuity with, not distance from, the children they bear.

Mary Condren discusses the assumption, found in different forms in ecclesiastical and some feminist theory, that women are by nature more peaceful than men. She shows that the historical record about the role of women in warfare is ambivalent. While in some situations women have protested about war, women have nevertheless served war in ancillary ways, from nursing to serving as concentration camp supervisors. In some modern settings, women have been active combatants. And women have always played symbolic roles in warfare, as the 'pretexts for war', those that must be defended, the 'warrior's rest and recreation', as cheerleaders, or as sacrificial and proud mothers. Hence women cannot be 'natural pacifists'. Yet the involvement of women in war is a tragedy, because warfare generates the symbolic capital for patriarchal culture which undermines women's self-interest. Condren argues that the cult of motherhood, with its ideology of self-denial and sexual repression, encourages women to confuse 'national interests' with their own, even as it confirms the myth of female powerlessness. And women's powerlessness and selflessness prevents women from recognising the political nature of child-rearing practices. Condren notes research that shows the correlation between rigidly defined sex roles and institutional violence, and between women's loss of self and misogynistic sons. She holds that the myth of women's moral purity and their privatisation ensures the loss of mothers' control over what is most precious to them, the lives of their children. Thus women must suspect and criticise traditional notions that they are 'protected' by men and by war. Women's role in peace-making will arise, not from idealist or theological categories about women's 'true nature', but from the praxis of women's lives, a 'maternal thinking' that is not an inherent virtue but a moral activity. The conjunction of the personal and the political will emerge in a theology that is respectful of the actual interactions of women and men and their political and theological consequences.

The final essay in this section teases out the connections between the rape of mother earth and patriarchy. Catharina Halkes explores the relationship of mother earth to ecology and patriarchy. She reviews the ancient conception of nature as home and contrasts it with the mechanistic thinking that characterises modern understandings. She suggests that the idea of rule of creation in Genesis 1 becomes domination in a patriarchal framework, and argues for the need of a renewed creation theology today. This theology would reverence the contemplative dimension of the seventh day of creation, a view which is expressed in the interdependence and egalitarianism of feminist thought in which the world is seen as God's body. Halkes urges the overcoming of the historical time of patriarchy's domination of women, nature, and the body as we learn to live in a humane and convivial society. Through the subversive new strategies of protest on the part of those who are marginalised, the immanence of God in our world can be realised.

The section on the use of motherhood in religious language and symbolism is introduced by the essay of Marie-Theres Wacker. She offers a feminist reading of Hosea 11 as a response to the ideology of service and suffering endurance of her mother's generation of women in the Church. In contrast to the understanding of the word of God (and the human word *to* God) as exclusively male, her approach to the biblical heritage suggests how the critical insight of a feminist daughter can recast traditional ideas. She sees this text in the Hebrew Bible as a mirror of the patriarchal situation today in which the political, economic and sexual power of men has issued in sexism, racism, and the exploitation of the Third World by the First, legitimated in the name of the Christian God.

She points out that while this text is often viewed by traditional exegesis as the great song of the fatherly love of God for the son, Israel, the word 'father' is nowhere mentioned. Christian readers too quickly read back an alien spiritual or churchly meaning into the text. A feminist interpretation suggests that this text does not deal with a punishing and authoritative male father in relation to a wandering son but rather with God's motherly care and heartache over Israel. In God there is a conversation between mother and father, a conversation in which the motherly side of God has the last word. As Wacker draws out the implications of her reading, she questions the reduction of women to nature or biology, insisting that the issue is not of blood but of adoption, a different kind of strength and solidarity. In the symbol of God as mother of compassion, there is an apt analogy with the message of the cross. Wacker holds that in the symbol of God the mother, Hosea breaks through the patriarchal understanding of the God of power.

Jane Schaberg illustrates a feminist reading of the New Testament in her provocative discussion of Matthew's infancy narrative as a story, not of virginal conception, but of the rape of Mary and the illegitimacy of Jesus. She argues that both Matthew and Luke took for granted an oral tradition that Jesus was so conceived by Mary during the time of her betrothal to Joseph and that they added the theological interpretation of this religious and cultural scandal as blessed by the power of the Holy Spirit. She examines four elements in Matthew's text to validate her reading. The genealogy (in which the foremothers Tamar, Rahab, Ruth and the wife of Uriah are all outside the patriarchal order and involved in sexual activity which risks damage to the social order and their own condemnations), far from affirming the miraculous, leads the reader to see the divine concealed in the human and accommodated to human freedom. The marital and legal contexts with regard to betrothal, marriage, rape or adultery explain the actions of Joseph, a Torah-observing or just man, in the quiet home-taking of Mary and adoption of her child. The role of the Holy Spirit in which, as in the parallel literature, divine begetting does not replace human parenting but rather stresses God's power in all life and generation. Interpretation of Isaiah 7:14, where a woman who *was* a virgin conceived naturally, suggesting that while Jesus' origin *was* ignominious and tragic, the divinely willed Messiah shows the siding of God with an outcast, endangered woman and her child. Schaberg concludes that the text confirms God's action within natural events but outside the patriarchal norm.

The adaptive power of the figure of Mary, virgin and mother, within Christian tradition is studied by Els Maeckelberghe, who uses not only the experience/institution distinction but gender-specific analysis as well. She disputes as androcentric a recent psychoanalytic theory which holds that the cult of Mary arose because of women's need to express their sexual desire for the father, the desire to bear the father's child. This theory assumes the oedipal crisis for girls as well as for boys. Feminist research, however, shows that while boys experience the crisis of differentiation from the mother, continuity and attachment to the mother is more central for girls. Thus the institutional picture of Mary painted by white, male, celibate hands is important for men as an external object, while for women her attraction lies in continuity and identification. At the level of experience, Mary is an object filled with phantasies for men while for women she is both virginal exemplar and the woman with a troublesome son, who knows women's difficulties; she is the motherly friend. Maeckelberghe calls for women's experiential interpretation in the Church today so that Mary can become one of many friends in the conversation of the community of believers.

Ursula King widens the conversation about the religious constructions of the symbolics of motherhood in an analysis of Hinduism, a tradition rich in divine female imagery. She affirms the distinctions between human constructs and the reality of the divine and between female symbolism for the divine and the idea of divine motherhood as she sketches Hindu ideas of a mother of all created beings perceived as Mother Earth or the Great Mother. Less directly linked with physical birth, having children, this mother is rather the source of everything, who nurtures and sustains all beings. The name of mother is sacred in its application to India itself, to the Ganges, and to particular goddesses. And the mother's sustenance applies not only to the physical but to spiritual food as wisdom and energy. While the great mother of the world is seen as merciful and compassionate, nourisher and protector, benevolent and beautiful, she is also the origin of death and disease, terrifying and fearful. This polarity is especially apparent in the goddess Kali who is the 'mad mother', wild, frantic, and untamed, yet gracious and saving to her devotees.

King argues that calling the divine 'mother' while relating both good and bad motherly characteristics to ultimate reality is more satisfactory than an exclusively positive mother symbol. The ambiguity of divine motherhood in Hinduism indicates the inability of any mother to conform to the positive institutional ideal. No child remains dependent on its mother but is destined for separation and the independence of maturity. The implications of this symbolism for Christian theology centre on the multiple meanings of the mother symbol; its limitations lie in that it entails only one aspect of a woman's potential. Moreover, it raises the problem of using only parental images for God, since in adult life images of equality and mutuality, not dependence and helplessness, are needed.

In the final essay, Sallie McFague confronts these questions more fully in exploring the theological possibilities and limitations of the mother symbol for God in a Christian context. Over against the heritage of a male sky god, a patriarchal figure who defeats fertility goddesses and orders all things hierarchically and dualistically, she suggests the capacity of a model of God as mother to underscore the interconnectedness of all life. Like King, she insists that maternal imagery must not be sentimentalised (women are not 'naturally' loving, comforting, or self-sacrificing); nor should it be suggested that women who are not mothers are not true or fulfilled women; nor that human beings are perpetual children but rather are called to adult responsibility for the world. In spite of these qualifications, maternal symbolism offers profound awareness of the precious and vulnerable character of life as such. The physical act of giving birth, with its elements of blood, water, breath, sex, and food offers internal rather than external images of God in relation to creation. The nourishment symbolism of food for all can suggest, in contrast with an anthropocentric point of view, cosmocentric perspectives that entail the ecological sensibility so needed in our time.

McFague shows how the mother symbol overturns the dualisms of mind/body, spirit/flesh, humanity/nature, male/female as it implies that the world is God's body, that God is, in some sense, physical. Her imaginative model highlights the radically interrelated and interdependent character of all life, the necessity of a just sharing among human persons and with other species, and undercuts dualistic hierarchies in a contemporary Christian perspective.

The issue concludes with Gregory Baum's critical analysis of the letter of Pope John Paul II on the dignity of women. While affirming the letter's recognition that God is father and mother, that generativity has no gender, and that the male/female relation is not partriarchal but equal, Baum points out its inadequacies to women's real experience today, particularly to the presence of women in public life as a 'sign of the times'. While motherhood is one aspect of women's lives, Baum emphasises the multiplicity of charisms and vocations in both Church and society which God distributes among both women and men.

This issue of *Concilium* again seeks to approach the articulation of feminist theology not in traditional dogmatic categories but from a critical systemic analysis of women's socio-cultural and religious experience in a global context. In preparing the issue we discovered that the exploration of motherhood as experience and institution raises multiple theological issues that cannot be covered in one collection. Moreover, the contributors took their topics in new directions and elaborated implications that have surpassed our projections. A fuller exploration of important experiences and topics, on which the essays only touch (children's rights, the rights of lesbian mothers, sexual abuse and battering, reproductive rights, mothers under slavery, mothers as workers, prostitution and motherhood, mothers-in-law, grandmothers, motherhood in native American or aboriginal Australian dual-sex societies or prehistoric matriarchal religions), would shed new light and provoke fresh theological approaches to the topic. And we regret the absence of theological voices from Asia where hoped-for contributions did not materialise.

In analysing motherhood as experience, institution, and ideology from different disciplinary angles, the present essays nevertheless provide a rich resource for a critical and constructive theology. We hope that these feminist theological reflections on the experience, institution, and ideology of motherhood will convince *Concilium* readers that women's voices must participate in the development of any theology that promises truth, liberation, and well-being for all.

Anne Carr
Elisabeth Schüssler Fiorenza

PART I

Motherhood: Experience and Institution

Ursula Pfäfflin

Mothers in a Patriarchal World: Experience and Feminist Theory

All human life on the planet is born of a woman ... most of us first
know both love and disappointment, power and tenderness, in the person
of a woman.[1]

MY MOTHER would be the last person I'd want to talk to about problems
I was having with my husband, said a woman last week in our group.
Another said, 'Last week I told my mother about my divorce and she was
not shocked; she treated me as a grown-up woman.' This woman then read
out what she had written in her diary that morning describing how this
experience made her feel reborn. We meet one evening each week to develop
our own spirituality, which we have felt in ourselves for a long time. In the
Churches, in which we are active, hardly any of us feel uplifted by our
faith. Mother Church reflects the same ambivalence as our own mother in
a patriarchal world: we seek her longingly and often retreat back into
ourselves angry and disappointed—lost daughters from the outset.
Gradually and tentatively the group is making its way towards where we
can re-encounter the lost daughter in ourselves and start celebrating both
mother and daughter in the woman we are.

In her book *Of Women Born*[2] Adrienne Rich is one of the first writers of
the second feminist wave this century to explore the difference between the
experience of being a mother and motherhood as an institution. Since then
there have been a great deal of writing and feminist theory, particularly in
the areas of psychology, psychoanalysis, sociology, politics and theology.

These are some of the themes this literature tackles: the history of mothering and present-day family developments; the social division of labour between men and women and its link with the subordination of women in patriarchal structures; the different value given to production and reproduction work and the burden on present day mothers doing several jobs at once; women's, especially single mothers' increasing poverty worldwide; the growth of violence in families and in public; the frightening figures for sexual abuse of girls and women by their own fathers, grandfathers, brothers and husbands; birth control, abortion, sterilisation, gene technology; the catastrophic results of our increasing destruction of nature, the source of all life; how daughters, women and mothers figure in the image of God and church institutions.[3]

At first discussion centred on the worldwide repression and exploitation of women's power but it has moved on to making women aware of their own power and influence. If we break our submissive silence and raise our voices can we and do we want to find other more appropriate paradigms for women in theory and practice?

This question brings up one of the most important disputes in the discussion of mothering since the first women's movement in the nineteenth century: are women different by nature? Do we have essential female qualities, arising out of our biological femaleness that make us different from men in our psyche, body experience, social behaviour and ways of thinking? This could be a version of the classic view of the polarity between men's and women's natures, an argument which has been used to repress women so successfully. Women were held to be closer to nature because of their female cycle and ability to give birth. Matter, body, sexuality and pleasure were seen as hindrances to contact with God, in which spirit was what counted. The carnal led to sin and so women were given a lesser place in God's image. This was the theological legacy of Augustine and Thomas Aquinas. The story of the collaboration between the serpent—the evil one—and Eve—mother of all the living—to cause original sin sealed theology's blessing upon the women-hating biology and philosophy of patriarchal antiquity.

Of course feminists have pointed out this legacy's bias, thereby challenging its claim to validity. French feminists such as Luce Irigaray and radical philosophers such as Mary Daly hold that women's particular qualities have been hidden and damaged by this historical manoeuvre but are now reappearing through a radical liberation from androcentric structures. And yet we only have a vague general idea what form this liberated femaleness will take, but it is already showing its creative power.[4]

On the other hand the American sociologist Nancy Chodorow does not think that sex makes women's nature different from men's. 'Gender differences, and the experience of difference are socially and psychologically created and situated, just as are differences among women.'[5] She distinguishes between biological *sex* and culturally determined *gender*. Hence she does not think it is at all a matter of course that women should nearly always be the ones to take care of babies and small children. Why do women 'mother'? How does mothering come about in women today? Historically of course it developed from the change in working conditions created by capitalism. With the rise of the isolated nuclear family, mothers were increasingly excluded from productive activity in the community and relegated to mothering. Chodorow's thesis is that mothering is not inborn or natural, but induced by social structures and reproduced by psychological processes.

> Sex-gender systems organise biological and social sex and babies. A gender specific division of labour in which women mother and look after babies splits off the private domestic sphere. Biological sex is organised in terms of heterosexual marriage which gives men rights over their wives' bodies and their children. Together this division of labour and marriage organise and reproduce social sex or gender as an unequal social relationship.[6]

Women in industrial countries today are much more numerous in the labour market, have much greater access to education and training and increasing influence in culture, Church and politics. So why do women still have the main responsibility for the children? Why the overburdened 'superwomen', coping with a job, house, partner and children? And at the same time women are far more likely to seek medical advice or hospital treatment than men, because they suffer from depression, inner emptiness, uncertainty, guilt feelings, disappointment in relationships, bulimia, compulsive eating, anorexia and psychosomatic diseases. Psychotherapists, theologians and sociologists too, are trying to understand why this should be so. They are investigating the social, religious and personal dimensions of a system which Anne Wilson-Schaef calls the 'white male system', Mirjam Greenspan the 'patriarchal, capitalist system', and Chodorow and others the 'sex-gender system'.[7]

Classical and more recent psychoanalytic theory is being revised and re-formulated in terms of women's experiences. Chodorow also tries to understand the phenomenon of the reproduction of mothering through the theory, mainly developed in England, of object relations. Like Dorothy Dinnerstein she believes that the fact that both men and women have their first life experiences with a woman is the cause of later differences between the sexes and men's and women's worlds. From this early relationship they develop their attitude to themselves and the world. The first person the newborn baby relates to is the source of its survival. It depends on this person for the satisfaction of all its bodily and psychic needs. Without this person's constant presence, sympathy and recognition of its changing needs for closeness and distance, a baby girl or boy cannot integrate its many fragmentary first experiences. Thus it cannot built a coherent self, which it will need later in order to engage in adult relationships. So both girls and boys gain their life's first fundamental experiences from this first carer.

However these experiences are not straightforward; they are ambivalent. Every child not only gets attention and satisfaction but also experiences denial, separation and ambivalent behaviour from the person caring for him or her. This person is not usually the father or a man but the biological mother or another woman. Thus the mother has enormous power over her children in the personal sphere, whereas in the social and political sphere she is relegated to second-class status. Like Chodorow, Magrit Brückner regards this as the origin of later defences against ties to the mother and of her social undervaluing.[8] As the earliest representative of the world, women are seen as part of nature, as non-human and unpersons, the source of good and evil.

The specific form that mothering takes depends just as much upon identification processes with the mother and re-experiencing one's own childhood as upon social factors. The more powerless the mother's position in society, the less independence given to her role, the more mystical and irrational maternal power appears to the child and to the mother herself; she is sacrificed to this role and makes her children her own victims. This also operates in other ways. Because women as mothers are so powerful in fantasy, they must be 'belittled' in society.[9] Like Chodorow and Kinnerstein, Luise Eichenbaum and Susie Orbach also see the later divisions between men and women as caused by the fact that boys and girls have their first experiences of life with a woman, but are introduced very early into social roles, which are not only different but defined as opposites.[10]

As mothers, women produce daughters who then have maternal powers and needs—they want a child. These capacities and needs arise in and from the mother-daughter relationship. On the other hand, women as mothers (and men as non-mothers) produce sons, whose motherly capacities and needs are systematically nipped and squashed. Thus men are prepared for their future role in society, which is a less feeling one than that of women.[11]

The problem of masculine children is that in order to develop their manhood they must differentiate themselves from their first love, because she is a woman. Boys learn that they are not female, not a mother. Thus separation becomes the most important feature of male self-identification and leads to the denial and splitting off of feelings and parts of themselves called female: needs for relationship, feelings of dependency, weakness, empathy and tenderness. On the other hand, the girl's sexual identity is founded not on differentiation but on feeling her oneness and connection with her mother. Her problem is that she shares not only her mother's positive expectations but also her ambivalence towards her own sex.

> Mothers and daughters share a gender identity, a social role and social expectations. They are both second-class citizens within a patriarchal culture and the family. . . . Traversing the generations from grandmother to mother to daughter is a particular psychology which has its roots and its flesh in the experience of being female in a patriarchal culture. The social requirements of deference, submission and passivity generate many complicated feelings. Often women do not feel complete, substantial or good within themselves . . . They are fearful and guilty about their sexuality and their strivings for independence, nurture and power.[12]

Thus women's mothering is reproduced by the mother's overwhelming presence and the relative absence of the father or other male and the mother is idealised and simultaneously devalued, from one generation to the next. Men and women cannot meet as equal partners because the asymmetry between their private and public power maintains the institution of motherhood and systematically prevents such a meeting.

In her research into abused women, Magrit Brückner has shown that women who stay longest with abusing men are those who identify most strongly with images of femininity and motherliness. 'My thesis is that the phenomenon of violence against women in marriage is closely connected to the position of women in our society. Abuse of women is an extreme consequence of their position in a society which tolerates such violent relationships.'[13] She sees the Church and theology as sharing in the responsibility for this destructive cycle, because they sanction social images of women by religious symbols and trap real women between Eve the temptress and the idealised Virgin Mary. Long before Jahveh, goddesses were worshipped who embodied in their trinitarian form all life's ambivalences, from birth through the celebration of the erotic to the journey to the kingdom of death. In all the great religions they were successfully ousted by the One Almighty God. This meant that all religious symbolisation of female power and autonomy in its many forms was also suppressed. When women and mothers were denied rights in society they also lost their own spiritual forms of expression.

But Brückner and others also stress that we as women are implicated in dominant male behaviour through our involvement in the patriarchal structures of our society. All women, like all men, have the capacity to affect the form relationships take. She stresses that it is not enough to fill old images with new contents, but that we need time to seek new paradigms and symbols for ourselves. This is now happening worldwide in women's groups, both inside and outside the Church and in feminist theology. An essential demand made by Chodorow, Dinnerstein, Eichenbaum and Orbach is that men should be equally involved in child care and women equally active in professional and public life.

On the other hand, feminists who hold that women are essentially different from men want to create a new, post-patriarchal culture, politics, philosophy and spirituality. Women must first acknowledge how they are interwoven into the current social web, in order to heal the splitting it imposes between body and spirit, mother and daughter, saint and whore, living for others and living for self. In my view, a new paradigm needs not only to abolish the split between the male and female world, but also the still little-acknowledged rifts between women from different cultures, classes, races and religions, who have different historical experiences. It must embrace career women and women in working-class jobs, white women and Afro-American, Arabic, Hispanic and Asian women. If we take seriously what has been said above about culture and social conditions having a crucial influence on the formation of femininity and mothering, then of course now at last we must seek our sisters who are only gradually, but very clearly, beginning to raise their voices. It is time for us to listen to them and pay attention. We must realise that 'our mothers' gardens' are as different, diverse and creative as we their daughters are, the women and mothers of today'.[14]

We begin to understand how we ourselves have absorbed the deep hostility towards women from our culture and we express it in our behaviour towards ourselves, other women and our own mothers. We must learn, perhaps painfully, from examining ourselves and also from our encounters with women who are fighting for the same goals as we are. Feelings we had towards our own mothers of longing to be held and disappointment when they set limits also affect our feelings about spiritual and political mothers now we are adults. We are still fighting with the problem of over-expectation. Society still has not solved the problems we face in trying to take part in public life, do a job and look after our children all at once. At the same time there are organised campaigns against sexuality, abortion, and birth control. Cuts in public spending threaten to wipe out the benefits women and mothers have gained for themselves and their children during the second half of the twentieth century. Mothers do not need a campaign for 'life'. They are the ones who give life and always have done. But Eve's abundant life has too often been compelled to be exclusively for childbirth and submission. We cannot fail to be affected by this history. Women have not escaped the heavy damage done to human beings by our culture. Giving birth became a burden for women because it forced them to accept male domination in its many forms, to pursue male interests by female means. Herein lies the core of woman's complicity.[15]

What helps is the rediscovery of our desire to know, enjoy and change. Our memory excites us, we become aware of when and how our wills have been broken, how we have been put down. We can gather our personal and collective histories and weave them into a marvellous new web, of women who can be as different and individual as they will. The main threads in this web will be the interconnection of all forms of life, cooperation and mutual responsibility.

One of the most important symbols in women's literature, research, political organisation and theology is the network or web. The spider is redeemed from its patriarchal condemnation as an ensnaring, threatening mother. She is reconnected with one of women's oldest and most skilful arts. She is the spinner or spinster and weaver of material clothing and covering necessary to our survival. She also divinely creates and upholds the web of both micro- and macrocosm. Hence women derive a spiritual sense of being together in all their diversity. This is a spirituality bearing the stamp of every mother's most individual talent: her power to transform.

Translated by Dinah Livingstone

Notes

1. Adrienne Rich, *Of Woman Born* (New York 1976).
2. *Ibid.*
3. *Cf.*, N. Chodorow, *The Reproduction of Mothering* (Berkeley, CA 1978); *ibid.*, 'Feminism and Difference: Gender, Relation and Difference in Psychoanalytic Perspective' in M. R. Walsh (ed.), *The Psychology of Women* (New Haven/London 1987); D. Dinnerstein, *The Mermaid and the Minotaur* (New York 1976); Ch. Olivier, *Les Enfants de Jocaste* (Paris 1980); U. Pasero and U. Pfäfflin, (eds.), *Neue Mütterlichkeit* (Gütersloh 1986); J. Treblicot (ed.), *Mothering—*

Essays in Feminist Theory (Totowa 1984); J. Rijnaarts, *Dochters van Lot* (Amsterdam 1987); C. Keller, *From a Broken Web* (Boston 1986); H. Göttner-Abendroth, *Das Matriarchat 1—Geschichte seiner Erforschung* (Stuttgart 1988).

4. M. Daly, *Gyn/ecology. The Metaethics of Radical Feminism* (Boston 1979); L. Irigaray, *Unbewusstes, Frauen, Psychoanalyse*, International Marxist Discussion 669 (Berlin 1977).

5. N. Chodorow, in M. R. Walsh (ed.), *The Psychology of Women*, p. 250.

6. N. Chodorow, *The Reproduction of Mothering*, p. 19.

7. A. Wilson Schaef, *Women's Reality* (San Francisco 1985); M. Greenspan, *A New Approach to Women and Therapy* (New York 1983).

8. M. Brückner, *Die Liebe der Frauen: Uber Weiblichkeit und Misshandlung* (Frankfurt 1983).

9. *Ibid.*, p. 135.

10. L. Eichenbaum and S. Orbach, *Understanding Women* (Harmondsworth 1985).

11. Chodorow, *op. cit.*, n. 6, p. 15.

12. *Op. cit.*, n. 10, pp. 37–39.

13. Brückner, *op. cit.*, p. 11.

14. L. M. Russell, K. Pui-Lan, A. M. Isasi-Diaz, and K. G. Cannon (eds.), *Inheriting our Mothers' Gardens* (Philadelphia 1988).

15. C. Thúrmer-Rohr 'Mannerist—Eine Geschichte der Wissensverweigerung', *Frankfurter Rundschau* (25 April 1989), p. 13.

Mercy Amba Oduyoye

Poverty and Motherhood

THE JUXTAPOSITION of poverty and motherhood is so strange as to be almost offensive. Granted this response is the result of socialisation and may be dismissed as the internalisation of domesticating cultural norms. In this contribution I do not wish to debate this issue nor go into the economic discussions that link motherhood with population control and the debates on abortion, planned parenthood and responsible parenthood, as all these affect men as well as women. I therefore do not wish to link them to motherhood. What I am offering is a testimony which I believe will find resonance in many African women's souls.

I am Ghanaian and an Akan with both my parents and their parents on both sides belonging to mother-centred groups. My political and economic status in Akan structures depend on who my mother is. I am who I am because of who my mother is. I have no biological children but I am the first of my parents' nine children. Any Akan daughter will tell you what that means. I have not experienced motherhood but I know what 'mothering' means. I have accompanied my mother through her motherhood. Motherhood has not made my mother poor. *My mother is rich.* She has a community of people whose joys and sorrows are hers. I am rich because I have this community and hold a special place in it. I am not a mother but I have children.

To many ears this sounds folkorique, a glorification of a culture, sublimation of instincts and many such explanations. For me this is life. The Akan proverbs below are not just sayings, they are the heart of the wisdom by which the Akan live today and can be a guide even for the management of the political unit called Ghana. Mothering is a religious

23

duty. It is what a good socio-political and economic system should be about if the human beings entrusted to the state are to be fully human, nurtured to care for, and take care of themselves, one another, and of their environments. Biological motherhood embodies all of this for the Akan as for many African peoples. One proverb observes: 'When you catch a hen her chickens are easily collected.' Children are disoriented and fall easy prey when mothering is absent or inadequate. Another proverb puts it more emphatically: 'When mother is no more, the clan is no more.' It is the presence of a mother that keeps the Akan family together in that social system. 'A child may resemble the father, but a child belongs to the mother.' With such a high premium on biological motherhood and mothering as a principle of human relations and the organisation of the human community, to associate motherhood with poverty will need a very careful analysis and detailed substantiation. Mothering, biological or otherwise, calls for a life of letting go, a readiness to share resources and to receive with appreciation what others offer for the good of the community.

There are several folktales of periods of famine depicting the sacrifices of mothers in order to save their children and many proverbs that crystalise in a few words what motherhood demands of women. 'The tortoise does not have breasts, but she feeds her children.' 'However inconvenient the path to the nest the brooding hen will get to her eggs.' So women in Africa exercise motherhood against all odds. The quality of a sense of duty and fulfilment and achievement that must go with this determination to see another person become human, cannot be associated with poverty of understanding about the value of humanity. It may be exercised in the midst of abject lack of material needs and that makes it all the more a marvel that women continue to mother. Scarcely ever does one find a deliberate choice of childlessness among African women and furtherest from our understanding of life is to make that choice for economic reasons.

1. The penalty of motherhood

Dramatic change in the economic basis of life in Africa is what has led to the association of women with poverty. The system makes women poor by deliberately excluding them from what generates wealth. Mothers fall easy prey to this new approach to community life that is more individualistic and competitive. When children were seen to belong to the whole family, indeed the whole community, being poor was not necessarily the result of having children. Today it can be a cause. When a nation acts as a mother to its citizens the education, health and well-being of children are in the national budget and mothers are treated as contributing to the 'assets' of the nation. What is a nation without people to make it great? It seems such a trite observation but children do not 'belong' only to parents, children are assets of the whole nation. Poverty is put together with motherhood when women are penalised by state, religion and culture for becoming mothers. In cultures that do not understand the African concept of family and mothering, a woman who bears her traditional responsibility of mothering, including carrying financial responsibility for children of the family (even if they are her mother's children) is penalised because of Western ideas of adoption. She is considered 'single' when her home is full of human beings to be nurtured and loved. The survival of these children depend on her industry and doing this has nothing to do with biology. But it is an indispensable aspect of the mothering that human life needs in order for human community to be humane and creative.

In some Western societies, women with children who are not attached to men are penalised in all sorts of ways, while in others women have to prove they have no men in order to get state assistance for their children. The criteria is not the welfare of women and children but their relation to the androcentric laws by which most of humanity is ordered and governed. These androcentric legal provisions have difficulty recognising mothers as heads of households but choose to invent names like 'single mothers' suggesting they have stepped outside the norm of submitting to male authority. There are no single parents (men or women) in Africa, as such persons are recognised as integral to the African family. Women-headed homes of modern times have been created by the exigencies of migrant workers who are prevented by the laws of the countries where they give their labour and pay taxes from bringing in even those closest to them, spouse and children.

In Africa the instabilities of war and the disruptions of natural disasters, economic and political mismanagement often result in the disruption of whole communities and inexorably propel women into the situation of having to parent their children single-handedly. Stateless and homeless, they struggle to care for the people who have survived with them. The global economic order that operates a hierarchy of persons is able to turn a blind eye to certain categories of human beings deemed dispensable. There are people whose welfare is theirs alone, but whose labour when they can sell it, is bought for wages that cannot sustain life. Their salaries are determined by how much debt their governments have to pay, what structural adjustments are being made and how determined the governments are to pay the cut-throat interest on loans they borrow from the loan granting nations in order to feather nests of 'experts' and 'advisors' from the same countries. The whole family suffers, but the traditional expectations that women will be more caring and more compassionate puts the burden of the situation on women. They give until they have nothing more to share but their poverty.

2. The impoverishment of women

The impoverishment of women in Africa is an aspect of the impoverishment of the Third World which had remained undisclosed or ignored until women themselves made their voices heard. Whatever poverty women as mothers struggle with cannot be understood apart from the real poverty-maker, power, the inability to influence the decisions that condition one's life.

Knowledge is power, and women are kept ignorant of how and what political, military and economic arrangements are arrived at. Women are kept ignorant of what the drugs they take, or are made to take, do to their own bodies and to the environment. The sources and the processes of the food they cook and put before their families are often not revealed and if they are, the economic and political milieu of the producers are not made known. Even where the agricultural and industrial processes involve women, women become peripheral to the actual decisions, they are 'farm hands' and 'robots' on assembly lines. The whys and wherefores are not made known to women. Why would women submit to radiation, Depo Provera, sex selection and other hazards of contemporary reproductive technology and genetic engineering that invade and violate their bodies and therefore impoverish their sense of personhood by treating them as objects of research and experiments? In most countries it is women who are exploited in this genetic technology.

In Africa socio-cultural impoverishment is more evident as Western technological culture intensifies its claim to be *the* human culture and imposes its norms of what is legal and ethical on the rest of the world. Women in Africa do not fall into the category of the under-employed, if anything they are over-employed as none can claim a 40-hour week. That they are underpaid as statistics have it for women globally does not need to be debated, but over and above this is the phenomenon of being taken for granted, of not having one's labour enter the statistics of national production. Their labour goes undocumented and therefore in the contemporary way of looking at government spending, women are not numbered among producers and therefore are not recognised as entitled to consume any social services. When one speaks of the impoverishment of women in Africa, one is referring to persons whose physical labour is used to fetch them enough sustenance for themselves and their families, but who can no longer cope because the market value of their products have fallen or the land that they used to deploy has been appropriated by governments or acquired by those with big money for more 'profitable' enterprises. Such 'profits' do not profit women in Africa and states impoverished by international economic injustice that no longer have the means to sustain women's welfare are the poorer for this.

In West Africa women continued their traditional economic activities of farming, food processing 'fast foods', making and marketing of household requirements and long distance trade as a parallel to the Western economic institutions that absorbed the labours of West Africa men in what is known as the 'modern sector'. Women's development in West Africa has followed this line and more and more supplementary income-generating activities have been created. Women's economic impoverishment has led to a burst of creativity in domestic survival strategies. Creativity in this area is sustained by the hope that the situation will change for the better.

On the level of traditional cultural demands however, little has changed and it would appear there is no hope for changes that will restore what is dignifying for women and remove the cultural obstacles to women's humanity. The impoverishment of women that has resulted from the joint effects of Western Christianity and Islam, Arabic and African cultures is still being overlooked. In conflicts of cultural values, women's culture and women's welfare have always taken second place. The real roots of the impoverishment of women, socially and economically, are to be found in the materialistic Western culture with its androcentric laws and perspectives, for these reinforce African ones and together suppress and often eliminate women's welfare from their provisions.

I have heard pronouncements during population debates that tend to assume that only African and other southern cultures value children and put the onus on women (married women, that is women whose attachment to men are socially approved) to provide care for them. This however is not the case, as the biotechnology that makes surrogate motherhood and *in vitro* fertilisation possible is beginning to tell another story. Men everywhere are capable of demanding babies of their wives rather than adopting and 'mothering' one that needs parents. Scientists exploit women's bodies for these experiments which require loans which the men may not even help to repay. There are cases outside Africa where mothers have been deprived of land by husbands and then thrown out with their children to fend for themselves. The Asante proverb *eba a eka oni* 'when it happens (*i.e.* when children get into trouble) it affects the mother', can be illustrated in many cultures.

The androcentric world needs to have a continual flow of human beings, to carry patriarchal names and other naming systems. The androcentric world needs children to be born and socialised into citizens who will even lay down their lives for their country. This androcentric world expects women to be the producers of human beings, but the experience of women is that their own development and perception of humanness and the human community has to be set aside in order to be 'good women', serving the system. Material and economic poverty are the experience of many women. Material and economic poverty are the experience of many mothers. What makes the latter thoroughly unacceptable is that the system often shields the fathers from the 'poverty' that could be associated with their paternity.

3. A child belongs to the mother

The mother-centred Asante who say a child belongs to the mother also say a child is the mother's until it is born, then its welfare becomes a community responsibility. The mother-to-be however is protected by the community. She is aided by taboos that will ensure safe delivery and guarantee the health of the mother. Inability to transform this ancient wisdom into modern socio-economic terms is what is at the root of the economic impoverishment of women. The impoverishment of mothers, therefore is an indication of the inability of human social thinking to match our technological development. Human relations and development of norms of community life lag behind economic systems. Women have fallen victim to this human poverty of spirit which puts profits before people and interests before production. In the hierarchy of human needs reproduction of the human species has a very low priority, hence motherhood is not priced. States and other institutions have not found a way of mothering the human community, only women and biological mothers continue to see this mothering of the human race as a sacred duty. Being poor, women make their communities rich, they guarantee the survival of their families in the face of all odds. The many television pictures of mothers in famine and refugee situations tell the story more vividly than words.

4. God's economy

In planning how the earth's resources could be managed to sustain all creation, God was generous from the beginning. In the beginning all was good, for all was of God. The interdependence of all creation was built into the beginning and there were no 'trespasses', and trespassers for all appropriated only what was necessary for survival and none was, or felt exploited. Few such communities may be found in human history.

Exploitation among human beings is only matched by human exploitation of the rest of nature. Exploitation of women by the human community is mirrored by the exploitation of the humanity of mothers in families and in society through social norms and legal provisions. What we need to turn our attention to therefore, is the poverty of the human spirit that ignores the humanity of women as persons in God's Image and mothers as co-creators with God and imitators of God's management of creation.

In a mother's economy, abundant life and comfort for others preceeds her own. Injustice to mothers arises from economic management which does not provide for a mother's well-being and comfort beyond her needs as a child-bearer. Even then all is done for the sake of the child. Are mothers human in their own being or cared for only in so far as they perform the biological function of child-bearing? The injustice done to women generally and specially to mothers has often been described as the injustice we do to the generation to come by our wanton exploitation of the earth.

As World Bank and International Monetary Fund prescriptions bite harder into the economy of the Third World, so the face of poverty becomes clearer and clearer. When a poor country has to export more to already rich countries, it takes land from the poor, especially women, to grow what the North needs, not what mothers in the South need to feed children. When governments cut spending, schooling and health-care fall on families and all work triple-time just to be able to feed the children — so mothers eat last. When wages and salaries are frozen so that a month's earnings only suffice food for five days, husbands and children eat first. When foreigners buy their investments to put into 'productive' ventures they grow for export, they weave and sew for export, they assemble for export and employ men, young women, older women and lastly women with children; all of whom are paid unjust wages that bear no relation to transportation costs and rising food prices.

The anti-baby economy of the North is preached in the South, through these economic measures and quite overtly, since at least in one African country young women can only get employment in the formal sector if they can show that they are on an anti-motherhood drug. So the message is clear, if you do not want to be poor or become impoverished do not become a mother. In God's economy, the human being is a necessary and integral part. God gave the management of the earth to the Earth-beings that God created. Managing has become exploiting, except where mothers are concerned. To cope with the survival of the people whose well-being depend on her, a mother spends all her meagre wages, does extra work, or stops wage-earning if home-nursing is what is needed.

In Africa women will continue to do all these things and more in order to be mothers. They may not have many children to fill the earth but the deliberate no-child solution is not an option. The solution lies in better management of creation, the earth, the human community, the nation and the home by both women and men, rich and poor, North and South. The increasing impoverishment of human communities in the South cannot be reversed by calling attention to motherhood. Mothers in Africa know poverty, but for them the solution is a challenge to which they respond in innovative ways. The survival of the human race is a human responsibility, not just that of mothers. Motherhood gives our race the guarantee of survival. Mothers are not only to be honoured, they are to be empowered.

Marie-Thérèse van Lunen Chenu

Between Sexes and Generations: Maternity Empowered

NO-ONE WILL be surprised if I say that our family life—five children born between 1957 and 1964, and with an enlarged group of their own age often around them—was and remains the microcosm of a succession of disputes, challenges and shifts of value. The period was rich in change and debate: democracy, human science and an impassioned search for a renewed ethic for all human relations aided by the new possibilities offered by contraception for choosing the conditions of parenthood. In all of this, feminism is involved, both as cause and consequence.[1]

During the same time, arguments within the Catholic Church were also crystallising, bringing with them the dispute among believers—in the name of their experience of faith—over the three crucial points of 'sexual morality', the question of ordination to the ministry, and the full and unreserved recognition of women.

At the risk of indulging in some personal reminiscences, I want to try and retrace here my experience as an ordinary Catholic mother who gradually became aware of the fact that these debates affected, if not particularly her identity, at least her profound model, received from the family and still defended by the Church/institution, though at the expense of some distortion.

We can understand how much the experience of motherhood is indissolubly bound up with the elsewhere and the otherness of generations and sexes. In the vital melting-pot of 'transmission' we discover how much we carry: deep-rooted riches which we think we can transmit, 'deposits' which we think we must transmit, and then attachments and nostalgia, weaknesses and regrets, debts and guilts . . . these are the things that haunt us, whether we are man or woman, father, mother, children, betters.

Our generation has been affected more than others by the protests of a rising generation which has been in no way responsive to a formerly effective parental barrier of systems of authority and reference. Our own children, who otherwise presented us with our most happy experience and who appreciate the good fortune of shared family love, displayed very early their 'holy' horror of the elements of power and shared responsibility associated with it. Each one of them, arguing with us as people, helped and took part in the dialectic game of our encounters as a married couple and parents, and in these soul-searchings, when distraught, hurt or miserable, we must often take account of what is ill-placed, poorly accomplished, too weakly or too deeply ingrained from the time of our own childhood . . .

I may even dare to say that the Church was and still is for me an instrument of provocation even to the point of scandal. On the one hand because it makes its own pronouncements on the realities which concern us—maternity, femininity, paternity, parenthood, sexuality, nature, otherness and transmission, and above all because it 'organises' itself (justifying, validating and perpetuating itself . . .) according to a typology of paternity/maternity which appears more and more challengeable and of which the recent papal exhortation *Mulieris dignitatem* 'On the Dignity of Women' provides a pathetic example. But on the other hand, the Church has provoked me—particularly in an invitation which affected my sexuality, my maternity and my filiation—because it carries a biblical, evangelical and mystic revelation and tradition, and a symbolism which demonstrate—even so far as to subvert the roles—the same polarisations of desire and indebtedness, of giving and receiving, the same contrasts of similarity and differences, the same rotation of interdependence, as that which seeks to gain influence today as a moral code of human relations.

We women of today passionately seek to discover 'the hidden word'[2] beneath the patriarchal order. And this hermeneutic work[3], as much as our experiences and our analyses, gives rise to what many of us claim to experience as a scandal for our faith: the hiatus, even to the point of contradiction, which appears between the model of paternity/maternity which the Church still claims, and what we ourselves claim as a new moral code of sexual and parental relationships.

I am well aware that my deciphering work—and perhaps even some of my 'family stories'—will conspire against the passionate character maintained by our culture and our religion around maternity and the Marian cult. To seek to bring to light certain elements and functions which originate and are perpetuated in the heart of that particular cult is above all to uncover an almost indescribable confusion of links between them, designed to adorn the Mother, the Virgin, the Muse, the Madonna. So it is like finding—if you will pardon this figurative evocation—childhood ribbons and favours which stir and trouble us, garlands which encumber, banners which suddenly unfurl and enthral us . . . and those veils, those crowns which lead you, whoever you may be, to the foot of the steps, before the altar, the recess, the pedestal, the throne . . .

To evoke a maternity empowered by a moral code of relations between sexes and generations, and to see to what extent the message and the practice of the Church contradict each other, I have here chosen a rather hybrid method of stories, reflections and integrated analyses. So let me, with the same image, give some indication of its course. We will have to untie the triple knot which binds the maternal reference in order to present it simultaneously:

— as a unity encompassing the whole of femininity: an ontological vocation which absorbs, or subordinates all other possible choices.
— as a unity given by nature, virginity, reserve, refuge, paradise lost . . . It makes you suspicious, like misdeeds, separation, sex, distance. And to give greater importance to reproduction and transmission of the self (the natural order, tradition, morality, family, Church.)
— as a unity enclosed in its own primordiality and sufficiency. What can this maternity really have to do with man, since it invalidates him as partner and as father, and leads him to the violence of patriarchal 'abduction'[4] at the same time as it keeps him devoted to her, consoled by temporal power—clerical and ministerial? And she accepts the sacrifice for herself, this great Virgin-Mother[5], reigning over the limited and opposing powers of sons/masters and submissive daughters prepared for maternity.

As we see, it is always the sexual division that we have to deal with, that is 'an artificial and symbolic division of the procreative power of the twin attributes of the two sexes'.[6] The uneasiness today concerns us all, women, men, children, faced with the definition of these attributes, and the organisation and functioning of the division.

1. Maternity/transmission

Being researched (even spied on?) oneself as a parent, one probably becomes more aware of how much one has remained the child. Whereas this age group which urges us on (wider than our own biological filiation)[7] is interested—sometimes losing interest!—in what we want to hand on, and where we got it from, as well as in the laws and rights of transmission.

In his 'Feminine Future', Jacques de Bourbon-Busset honours the 'women who accept their vocation as mothers . . . instead of rejecting it', thus becoming 'the framework of societies and civilisations'.[8] 'Woman receives life and transmits it, and through this mission . . . this mysterious work which is accomplished within her, she works with God.'[9] By such pronouncements, of which thousands of examples in different registers can be found, we can measure how the division is made: the mother is presented as procreator, the father as creator (the sperm, symbolic order, the law, social and artistic development . . .), the woman as transmitter.

As for our own children, they soon understood that my undue sorrow at their questionings and my reluctance to appreciate and discuss their meaning, were linked simultaneously to my mother, to morality and to my faith. My mother was tender and good; my parents loving partners who did not conceal the fact. I was just as cross with my mother for trying to impose on me another theoretical and social code. When I was about to marry, she said to me: 'Do whatever you like, but always arrange things so as to leave him thinking that he is in command.' (I had had a deep-seated hatred from a very young age of this game of scorn and occult powers played between the sexes; it spoiled some adults for me . . . and earned me a few smacks for my impertinence!) Twenty years later, at the age of forty, I was on holiday at my parents' home when one of my over-spontaneous observations caused my mother, for the first time in front of me, to lose control of herself. I had said: 'For a kidnapper, that man is rather likeable.' She retorted: 'If you can think that, then you're no daughter of mine!' I was frightened by this for a long time, delving deep into my wonderful childhood memories in order to rid myself of other sources of blackmail which may have been lurking there. My children often had to dislodge me from my entrenchment behind the barricades of transmission at that time . . . They would say to me: 'You're not giving the orders any more but you're tired or you're crying . . . and that comes to the same thing!' (Oh, Saint Monica, what virtue had we not ascribed to the tears of the Christian mother!)

2. Maternity-femininity-maternity

My two daughters came home from school revolted, a year apart almost to the day. Yet they had had their religious lesson, and with a good text. The lesson for the day was: 'Man and woman, two vocations; God created woman for maternity.' This 'for' really got through to them. And I had to reinforce them in Christian awareness and in their own identity as women, as I had so often to reinforce myself. Created, my sisters, my daughters, created by the will and love of God. There is nothing else to be received; and received with man, as a gift and responsibility, to manage children and call them to life. It is not the woman *for*, it is the woman who can. Wonderfully!

3. Giving life?

This was how I was introduced recently to 200 priests who had come on a day's retraining course: 'Our lecturer today has brought five children into the world.' This gave me the chance of a delightful retort: 'Ah, at least we don't have to teach you the specific nature of woman!'—'Tell me, anyway.'—'She gives life.'—And what if it was man *and* woman,—equal inheritance of will, of welcome and of genetics, competing equally, and equally responsible for the creation of life? And if I were to say how much I rejoice that the power of the mysterious alchemy of the womb is past . . . And if I told you—because I *know* it—that a child takes his life and comes into the world through a mother who parts herself!

A fine symbol, in truth, and a real contingency. We are the sea which parts to give passage, uplifted with joy to the pleasure of discharging, of reaching one's term! Torn, shattered, seeking restoration . . . We are also the theatre, the play, the audience and the actors, a mother, a father, amazed to be introduced to Life! Imposing, fragile, temporarily committed in a stream of pride and tenderness. I was there, astounded by the direct share of the father, seeing and greeting, before me, that child whom I did not know either, whom he had also expected, imagined and held in his arms. Astounded also by the share of other people. The solidarity of friends and family, the quality of the concern, the enthusiasms of a team for this great match of life, all share in the festive welcome: a significant initial way of marking that the child does not 'belong' to his family. Social solidarity also for this life which must be separated from itself by the knife of distance; the trace of which is carried in the centre of every human being. Separation from the mother? Of course . . . separation also from its own envelope, a placenta which is genetically and biologically its own. Separation also from all that is said about maternity: 'It seems that the Judaeo-Christian societies are those which place the greatest emphasis on the "vector uterus", almost going as far as to confuse maternity and pregnancy-labour. Similarly, they have fixed paternity in the single sperm of fruitful coitus'.[10] To deny 'the paroxysmal inflation of the role of the mother in childbirth', to produce 'the hidden face of the parent-to-be: the role of the father'[11], to recognise the extraordinary similarity of the illusions and even the psychological behaviour of men and women in the face of procreation, is to submit ourselves mutually to a high degree of asceticism concerning our sexual roles and at the same time for each parent to train himself—the one enabling the other—to regulate the right distance from the child. He will not grow except by adjusting this distance to the point of stretching it and sometimes cutting it before being able to replace it. It is therefore his adult choice, incomprehensible for us, painful for us as for him . . . in which we can only accept being distanced and not abandoned. Trust has been established. Unshakeable solidarity has been revealed. Humour can exist between our awkwardness and his: 'You know, you have seen, I'm only an ordinary little mother . . . But you only have one . . .'

Does being father or mother make any difference here? We do not know exactly, but we know how difficult it is for a child to situate himself *vis-à-vis* a father or mother who is an object of veneration. Pregnant father, 'father hen', 'new father', single mother, parents in all the new combinations, as well as the normal ones, not forgetting all the spiritual fathers in the world, we have to ponder these words of the mother in *Eden Eclaté*: 'I touch with my finger the lie attached to our origins. Is it the child or I who has more greedily drunk at the maternal springs? Is it the foetal child or the embryonic mother who has lost herself in the tranquillity of the womb?'[12]

Not having known how to interpret maternity except in terms of sacrifice/virtue/holiness . . . the Church has failed to understand (and *Humanae vitae* demonstrated this) that the choice not to have a child might be a noble one. It has also failed to seek sufficient support in the work of human sciences to enable it to establish an ethical code which does not uniquely concern maternity but which might fittingly be a valid model for it in so far as it would not be isolated from other interpersonal relationships. Instead of enclosing man and woman, father and mother, within closed or narrow 'specifications', one might propose, as a basis for this ethical code, the undermining of certain knowledge which has become power . . . the dispossession of certain complacency so that each partner might empower the other, and practise the open inter-play of exchange.

This goes beyond the process of dialogue. It is not a question of tempering the paternalism and materialism which remain, but of allowing the freedom of the other to exercise itself to the point where it deepens, examines and partly reformulates the content of transmission, which then becomes like an open summons to the creativity of interpersonal dialogue with relevance to the signs of social history.

A quite different conception of ecclesiastical dialogue, of the fixed 'content' of the revelation and of the authoritarian role of the Magisterium is shown in the recent Apostolic Letter of John-Paul II *Mulieris dignitatem* 'On the Dignity of Woman and her Vocation'[13] Here we see the institution/Church functioning simultaneously as a timid wife and as an embryonic mother . . .

4. On the maternal dignity!—of the woman

Clearly, the framework of this article does not permit a sufficiently extended analysis of this last text. At least we should seek out the current official teaching of the Church on maternity. From the parameters drawn in this article, I will propose three keys to reading it:

— the Letter shows that official theology borrows from several anthropological schemes which partly cancel each other out.
— rather than drawing conclusions from its statements on the equality of the sexes, for the benefit of its own ecclesiology and in order to produce a more acceptable ethical code of sexuality, it is more concerned with developing *the vision which it has of itself as bride and mother*, according to anthropological models which are currently under challenge.
— this apologetic concern, this closed and authoritarian centralism, can explain the systematic character of the reasoning which relies on *elements which are separated* from their semantic context. Thus the Letter appears in the end—and this despite its new elements which are valid in themselves—as an unconvincing attempt to re-centre a teaching which does not respond to the demands of thought and ethical values today.

(a) Anthropological foundations

As we know, the Letter at first provoked comments which were mostly positive, greeting as 'anthropological change'[14] the affirmations which come from what we might call the new schema of 'joint reciprocity' between the sexes. They are well formulated and rely on open and interesting re-readings of the Bible; they were even described as 'a feminist re-reading of the Bible by John-Paul II'[15]. It is a matter of placing ontologically 'the unity of the two . . . called from the beginning to exist . . . one for the other' (n. 7), 'in reciprocal submission . . . mutually trusting each other' (n. 14). 'In the human order', the Pope specifies, the begetting of children 'is the special gift of the unity of the couple, the man and the woman beget children'.

There we are in harmony with the development of the Rights of Man and their recent expression, notably in the *United Nations agreement against all forms of discrimination against women.*[16]

Alongside this schema exists another, which I will term 'Christian patriarchal', thus indicating the adjustment—quite prophetic in its time—of the order of masculine precedence in such a way that the *submission* of the woman is accompanied by her *equivalence* with man;[17] in our century are added those steps taken to revalue woman around a 'theology of femininity'. A characteristic of this 'classic' schema is the polarisation between activity/passivity or receptivity, and precedence/'equality—but . . . .'. And obviously, the nuptial symbol is related to this. Before restating what consequences remain for the functions within the Church, let us show here a few traces of the prejudices relating to this typology: 'It is the woman who receives love, and loves in turn' (n. 29).

The third schema, very favoured in this text, goes ever further back: that of the 'phantom-mother at the dawn of civilisation and at the dawn of all our lives . . .',[18] that of 'maternal primordiality': 'Man must learn his own paternity from the mother' (n. 18); 'He is placed in woman's hands' (n. 30). It is a schema of 'nature' since it embraces the personal dignity of woman within the maternal vocation (woman created 'for' . . .); there is collusion between a possible existential vocation and the essential vocation. Maternity, then not empowered by sexuality, is surrounded by a sort of aura of matricentric sacredness, if by that we indicate that unity of power of pre-Christian myth. Validation is here sought in a recourse to a deified Mary[19], who becomes the archetypal woman: '*the fulness of grace* granted to the Virgin of Nazareth in view of her quality as "Theotokos" signifies at the same time *the fulness of perfection of "what is characteristic of woman"*, *"of what is feminine"*' (n. 5., underlined in the text).

(b) What Church?

The vision of the Church only seeks its foundation here in the nuptial symbolism, introduced by the caption 'the Great Mystery'. From the viewpoint of the strong affirmation of man/women reciprocity, the use which is made of it here can only appear as even more literal and compliant. We see the disparity in the treatment of certain texts according to whether they concern men or women. Let us give two examples: Christ is presented as *the archetype of man* ('The symbol of the bridegroom is masculine') (n. 25); Mary is the *archetype of the dignity of woman* (n. 25). Man can be placed, like woman, under the sign of the Bride, the figure of humanity, the figure of the Church, and both participate in the 'unique priesthood of

ᐟ
the baptised' (n. 27); whereas only man can signify the Bridegroom. This disparity between man and woman relates to the twin perversion of the submissive woman (the real woman) and the sacred woman (the Church) and, more generally, to the primordiality of her 'supreme vocation' (n. 31); 'Christ counts on her to accomplish the royal priesthood' (n. 30). We would seek in vain for other symbolism which relates to Christic theology—race, body, community—...[20] The sacredness of Mary becomes all-embracing and hovers over a Church maternal rather than spousal, and which proclaims itself as 'Marian' as well as apostolic and 'Petrine'.

(c) Disjunctions

These underline the apologetic nature of such teaching. There will be an abundance of *semantic shifts* (symbols or analogies extrapolated in conceptual declarations, for example 'The truth about woman as wife . . .'); *unexplained juxtapositions, unfounded antitheses* ('compared with man', 'compared with God', 'the human order', 'the order of love', 'the particular value of the woman as a human person', her 'prophetic character . . . in her femininity'). Whilst the whole text suffers from an uneasy disjunction between *the affirmations of principle* and *their consequences* which remain ignored; the text's status is affected by the disjunction made by the Pope between *his personal reflections* and the document containing *the conclusion of the Synod* from which this question of the Church in relation to women was eradicated.

Those men and women who had thought that our old socio-cultural and religious heritage of androcentrism and misogyny was enough to explain the obstructions placed before women by the Institution/Church should ask themselves if this text does not reveal another, more archaic, reason: the inordinate conception which the Church has of its vulnerability as a Mother! That would be like a Roman mother, on the defensive, with Marian dogmas, rather more than the active and conciliar wife, the community and the Body of Christ in the signs of the times: 'Pilgrim, called *Marialis Cultus*, hastening towards the Holy City.' We were not expecting the Message to be on the Church, but on the recognition by the Church of women and of the man/women relationship today. We see that the doubt, the solitude, the weariness and the exasperation of women, in the face even of violence and abandonment by their husbands, or in the face of the inadequacy of fathers, come together with other considerations (for example, the new techniques of reproduction) and these new models of child-as-fulfilment,   child-of-well-being,   child   which   successfully consummates the marriage, towards a temptation to re-centre the 'archaic' model of feminine/maternal imprisonment and sublimation according to current sensibilities, whereas the Church still plays its part by discourses like this, as well as by its own ecclesiastical practice of disjunction between men and women. Is it not time for us to seek together how to recognise our living differences and strengthen each other through dialogue and interchange of ideas—paternity/maternity remaining symbolic and at the same time very real models? It seems to me that only equality, mutual strengthening and a denial of gratification can help us to write new stories of wonderment and solidarity between the sexes and generations and, dare I say, between couple and family.

Translated by Barrie Mackay

Notes

1. In its objective sense as social or historic movement.
2. M. P. Defossez, *La Parole Ensevelie* (Paris, 1987).
3. E. S. Fiorenza, *En mémoire d'elle; essai de reconstruction des origines chrétiennes, selon la théologie féministe* (*Paris 1987*); ET *In Memory of Her* (London 1987).
4. S. Blaise, *Le Rapt des Origines ou le Meurtre de la Mère*, published by the author (Paris 1989).
5. M. Warner, *Seule entre toutes les femmes, mythe et culte de la Vierge Marie* (Paris 1989) ET *Alone of All Her Sex* (London 1976); Group for Interdisciplinary Research into the Study of Women, *Générations de vierges* (Toulouse 1987).
6. G. Delaisi de Parseval, *La Part du Père*, (Paris 1981) p. 288.
7. I am here drawing on my own experience: heterosexuality and a family relationship. These are not models which exclude all other choices.
8. In *La Croix* (14 December 1985).
9. Mgr. L-A. Elchinger, 'La vocation permanente de la femme', in *Je Plaide pour l'Homme* (Paris 1976).
10. G. Delaisi, *op. cit.*, p. 289.
11. *Idem.*, p. 15.
12. A. Pilon Quiviger, *L'Eden Eclaté* (Quebec 1981).
13. French edition (Paris 1989); the numbers in brackets refer to the numbers of the paragraphs.
14. *La Croix* (14 October 1988).
15. *Le Monde* (1 October 1988).
16. M. Th. Van Lunen and L. Wentholt, 'Le statut de la femme dans le code de droit canonique et dans la convention des Nations Unies', in *Praxis juridique et religion* (Strasbourg 1984) 1, pp. 7–18.
17. K. E. Børresen, *Subordination et equivalence; nature et rôle de la femme d'après Augustin et Thomas d'Aquin* (Oslo, Paris 1968).
18. Gabrielle Rubin, *La phantasmère ou les sources inconscientes de la misogynie* (Paris 1977).

19. R. Laurentin, *Court traité sur la Vierge Marie* (Paris 1967).
20. S. Tunc, 'L'égalité des baptisés, enjeu pour l'Eglise', Document: *Femmes et Hommes dans l'Eglise* (Paris 1988).

Ivone Gebara

The Mother Superior and Spiritual Motherhood: From Intuition to Institution

THIS IS a broad, complex and varied subject, which can be approached in a number of different ways: from a historical, psychological, cultural, religious, sociological or other standpoint; starting from the past or from current experience in different places. This study, though using elements from the European past, seeks mainly to show the changes taking place today both in the function of a Mother Superior and in the understanding of spiritual motherhood, particularly in certain sectors of the Church in Latin America. My main approach is theological, but taking account of other implications.

I start from the thesis that the basic nucleus around which spiritual motherhood in religious communities has been elaborated is deeply patriarchal. The spiritual motherhood practised by women consecrated to God, despite expressing different aspects of feminine existence, has been patterned on the idea of a model desired by God the Father, the organiser of all that exists. As a result, the basic orientation given to this motherhood starts with the authority and power structures obtaining in society and in the hierarchical-clerical Church.

I go on to show how criticism of the present model of Western society, of the hierarchical and patriarchal structures of the Church, and the growth of the feminist movement are contributing to rejection of the traditional role of the Mother Superior and the concept of spiritual motherhood. This is now leading all religious, but women religious in particular, to thirst for meaning and to look tirelessly for new ways of living their vocation, in an attempt to revivify the institutions that were once the glory of a particular church tradition. The future has posed its challenge: looking and listening to the 'signs of the times' and interpreting them correctly are both a call and a need for us all.

This study is divided into three mains sections:
— 1. Spiritual motherhood and the body;
— 2. The iconoclasts of spiritual motherhood;
— 3. The new role for spiritual motherhood.

1. Spiritual motherhood and the body

It is important at the outset to note that speaking of spiritual motherhood includes a consideration of motherhood as a basic vocation for women. This viewpoint has always seemed to most people a fact inherent in the 'nature' of women, something without which they cannot be faithful to the order laid down by God. Woman and Mother are, from this viewpoint, virtually synonymous. Furthermore, to be a mother is in a way to recover and redeem the 'fallen' nature of woman, an attempt to overcome the 'sin' of Eve and her daughters.[1]

In communities of women religious, motherhood has always been a positive value, even though sublimated and spiritualised. But the same cannot be said of the body; this has been a reality to be feared and fought, the setting for temptations of the devil and infidelity to God. Women's 'natural vocation' to motherhood has even in some way been opposed to the weak and dangerous reality of the body, leading consecrated virgins to practise and speak of 'spiritual motherhood', thereby bringing together women's essential calling and their calling to spiritual holiness.

In this way, consecrated virgins became 'spiritual mothers' with the power to beget—spiritually—daughters and sons for God through the gift of their lives and the conscious immolation of their bodies. Many groups of women religious spoke of spiritual motherhood as the gift of making someone be 'born again' to life with God, of leading someone to the good, of taking in those despised and abandoned by society. Such a function or mission, seen as maternal, was for centuries regarded as a higher degree of perfection than simple physical motherhood.

Spiritual mothers entirely dedicated to God celebrated their symbolic nuptials with the Son of God. They were virgin brides of Jesus Christ, his followers, servants, sometimes called daughters or sisters, as attested by the immense variety of names given to religious congregations as they came into being over the course of the Christian centuries.

As we know, the concept of spiritual motherhood as a value of the highest order emerged in the Christianity of the early centuries.[2] It was marked by an androcentric and theocentric view of the universe, and also by a deeply dualist view of human nature, which lasted for many centuries and still persists today in some Churches and religious communities.

Spiritual motherhood became an institution and received its legitimation in the Catholic Church, just as biological motherhood receives its legitimation and social recognition in the Church through the sacrament of matrimony. Its legitimation is achieved through the three main religious vows, of poverty, chastity/celibacy and obedience, made in public according to the requirements of Canon Law.

From the point of view of this study, the important thing to note is that these vows, the style of life, of dwelling, the type of human relationships, the language used, the submission to a Church governed by men, all for centuries upheld a form of spiritual motherhood that expressed a world view rooted in so-called eternal and spiritual values. So it implied renouncing the world and its pleasures, along with family ties and friendships made earlier. One's body, the seat of spiritual conflict, was not something to be obeyed; its desires, attractions, emotions, seemed to contradict the movement towards God, towards the heights of the Spirit, towards the 'most elevated' aspirations. The body was an ever-present temptation. There was no alternative but to live with it, on one's guard against its possible traps. So one had ceaselessly to imitate 'the purity of an angel in a sincere and perfect clarity of body and spirit'.[3]

A spiritual mother became ever more perfect to the extent that she overcame the limitations of her 'material' body, to the extent that she approached the angelic ideal. To this end, fasting, cilices and various spiritual exercises were not only permitted, but recommended by spiritual directors in confession or by the superior of the community.

In this context, the Mother Superior was responsible for ensuring the conditions necessary for every sister or 'mother-religious' to be able to live the spiritual ideal set forward by the institution. Therefore, the obedience owed to the Mother Superior should be a mirror of obedience to God, seeing that she represented the will of God in the community. This submission had to reach the depths of one's soul, requiring the novice or permanently professed sister to examine her conscience on her attitude to the Mother Superior. The *Miroir spirituel de l'âme religieuse*, dating from the end of the nineteenth century, gives a classic example of this: 'Have I considered the novice mistress as being in God's place where I am concerned, and, from this viewpoint, have I the deepest respect for her, never speaking of her in a way that might do her harm, closing my eyes to her faults, treating her with all the deference and respect due to the position entrusted to her?'[4]

Spiritual motherhood could produce fruits only under the strict control of not just the authors of the scheme, but also of the Mother Superior herself—a sort of Super-Mother, understanding and kind, but equally demanding and tough when the institution seemed threatened by behaviour considered deviant in relation to the ideal pursued. There were not infrequent times when this Mother became a Stepmother and 'daughters' felt themselves orphans, when welcome was turned into abandonment, when the divine ideal was replaced by a lust for power. And often the Mother had recourse to 'Father' to impose his views on the world and human relationships on her 'daughters'. Priests were those who knew the 'truth about God' and the best way of doing his will.

The ideal of spiritual motherhood was a 'patriarchalised' ideal: that is, the ideal Mother was worked out in terms of 'Father's' orders and approval, and furthermore, in accordance with the virtues and ascetic practices recommended by 'Father'. The low regard in which women were held on account of their bodies was a reflection of the threat posed by Eve's body to the clergy who held spiritual power. This is why 'spiritual directors' recommended paying special attention to the area of chastity of body and mind, avoiding seeing and being seen, desiring and being desired. Living in chastity was not only a virtue and a security for religious themselves, but also for others a safeguard against that 'enemy' with its pleasing, seductive and attractive appearance: women's bodies. All this, of course, was experienced as a value and a truth, in a sort of quiet acceptance of a world organised in a particular manner, in which everyone had a precise place in the existing, hierarchical order of things.

Within this scheme of things, one must remember that, with a few exceptions, the total handing over of one's life to this sort of religious community was the expression of a genuine attitude of love of God and following the teachings of Christ. These were the reasons for accepting sacrifices, sufferings and humiliations. One lived in the conviction of a 'greater joy' beyond present suffering, in the conviction that this profession of faith and 'mad love' of God were seeds of redemption for the human race. Theological outlook and world view justified this style and choice of life which, without doubt, led women of singular qualities to missionary presence and activity in places abandoned and forgotten by public authorities in all corners of the world. Their hands dried tears and cured wounds; their feet trod paths to the poor and marginalised; their dedication to God's work is a witness to an unending love.

2. The iconoclasts of spiritual motherhood

Winds and storms arose to shake inherited certainties. Walls fell on all sides; images were destroyed, convictions shaken, beliefs lost. Values defended in the Middle Ages and re-entrenched in a certain 'modern' mentality were called into question. A mounting cyclone seemed to be blowing up, causing a great shutting of doors and barring of windows so as to maintain eternal values, defend the purity of ways of life, keep the integrity of particular customs. The rising storm threatened to do away not only with the motherhood of women in general, but institutionalised spiritual motherhood in particular.

Who are these iconoclasts, and what these threatening storms? 'Devils' for some and 'prophets' for others, they have various names. Let us mention just three, which embrace others: critique of the present model of Western society, critique of the hierarchical and patriarchal model of the Church and its theological underpinning, and the world-wide growth of the feminist movement. These devils or prophets hold hands with one another, work together, and seem to be getting stronger and ushering in a different future. As we approach the end of the century, they proclaim a qualitatively different world, despite the continuance of old structures.

In Latin America above all, it began with the poor. These began to affirm their existence, to overrun politics, states, economies, universities, churches and even religious congregations. Their growing number and the clamour of their shrill voices, claiming living space for themselves, began to cause alarm. A stench rose from their destitution and no political 'deodorant' could prevent it from growing and spreading. Their deaths, their lives, the increasing numbers of their sons and daughters threw out scientific forecasts, confounded calculations and researches. The life of the poor imposed itself as a historical fact, as the shameful affirmation of a society built at the cost of thousands of dead, of the destruction of the environment, and of the exhaustion of the patience of men and women of good will. The cries of the poor managed to penetrate some institutions, not always with the force they hoped for, but strongly enough for their situation to be recognised by the community of nations and for some things to begin to change.

'Fathers' left their sacristies and 'Mothers' their convents: the hour of justice had struck; there could be no place for spiritual fathers and mothers while 'their children' were dying of hunger. All were brothers and sisters united in the same goal: to fight the causes of death of the poor of Latin America.[5] And God, 'He' who had kept them apart from the world and protected them as his 'property', now seemed to 'change his mind'. He sent them out to fight in the world, to struggle against the social forces of evil. It was a new 'holy war'; the enemies of the poor were God's enemies too.

To build a new world, new men and new women, starting from the poor—this was the order of the day. No one had time any longer to think about spiritual fatherhood or motherhood. The 'time' had come: why wait until the morrow, why talk about eternal values in the face of the massacre of human lives? Why think about the afterlife when it was scarcely possible to live from day to day in this one?

Faced with this picture, spiritual mothers gave up their honorific titles. Now they used just one name like everyone else, accepting the prefix 'sister' at most. Their bodies, dwellings and life styles began to reflect the desacralisation of their world. The deep changes taking place in their lives at first caused bewilderment among the poor themselves, used as they were to solemn figures belonging to a world based on the sacred. For professed religious, everything took on a new meaning. Those for whom they lived and struggled were now much closer, with faces, hearts, classes, smells, bodies. So their spiritual motherhood had to be relocated, along with so much else in their lives.

This first devil or critical prophet went together with another, which made its special task to sweep away the hierarchical and patriarchal model of the Church, and consequently the relationship of submission of 'spiritual mothers' to the holders of 'spiritual power'. It was seen that the same society that 'produced' the impoverished, also 'produced' a hierarchically-structured, male-dominated religion. Nevertheless, 'sacred' organisation was difficult to strike at, since it possessed subtle and powerful arms with which to impose its will as the will of the Most High. Despite this, its body was struck by the 'cyclone'; a wound was opened, and has proved difficult to hide. It will continue to grow till the body is changed and new flesh can be born.

Its theology, reflection on God and the 'things of God', is being questioned. It cannot go on legitimising a religious society which proclaims justice for others but fails to practise it itself. It cannot go on speaking of 'man' in general, forgetting women, different ethnic groups and the minority cultures spread around the globe. It no longer has the power to impose a spiritual motherhood based on the patriarchal model and to justify it on the basis of a-historical, other-worldly ideas, treating the metaphors of other ages as reality.

Finally, the third devil or prophet, called the 'feminist movement'. This has helped to produce the progressive decline of the patriarchate within women's religious communities and to create new ideas on man-woman-nature-power-divinity-salvation relationships. The great majority of 'religious' women now feel the urge to rethink their theological understanding, to place it under a light other than the one that was imposed on them as the only one capable of lighting their lives. The present time is one of uncertainty, of instability, of suffering, but it is an extremely creative time.

In this situation, where does spiritual motherhood stand? Will the historical evolution of this last part of the twentieth century spell the death of this type of motherhood? Is it perhaps saying that the whole tradition of begetting 'sons and daughters' for God, the inheritance of an age-old tradition, is doomed to disappear? Could spiritual motherhood be ceasing to be the 'privilege' of consecrated virgins living in religious communities? These questions will be examined in the third section of this study.

3. The new role for spiritual motherhood

'Rejoice, O barren woman who have not given birth; sing and shout for joy, you who never had children, for more are the children of the rejected woman than the children of the married wife . . .' (Isa. 54:1).

Today in Latin America, the frontiers of spiritual motherhood are broadening out. We speak first of de-institutionalised 'spiritual mothers' . . . Who are they? Who are these women with numerous offspring, who beget though barren, who beget without 'knowing man', who beget as virgins?

In the first place, they are leaders of the people, wise woman whose close connection with life's realities enables them to listen to, feel for, advise and help those (of both sexes) who come to them. They are those who without title, belonging to no officially recognised institution, 'widen the area of their tents' in order to provide their share of love for the process of building life. They have always existed throughout history, but as socially 'absent' beings, as people of no importance whose existence was not worth adverting to. These women—widows, married, single parents, with few or numerous dependents—exercise a 'spiritual motherhood' among the people without giving their daily gift of life, their begetting of the Spirit, this or any other name.

Poor themselves, bound up with the daily lives of the poor, tested through the same sufferings, knowing their dreams and hopes, such women are capable, in diverse ways, of alleviating the orphanhood of the people. It might be through time spent with a neighbour, the offer of a pot of tea, or through leading a neighbourhood association or a women's group, that they exercise what I am calling 'spiritual motherhood', taking the term in a wider sense, modified by the demands of life itself. And alongside them, sharing their approach to life, are professional women, intellectuals, political militants and religious committed to the impoverished, capable of 'loving their neighbours as themselves', capable of leaving 'descendants as numerous as the stars in the sky'.

And what of the role today of those who have inherited the institutionalised form of 'spiritual motherhood'? Are they to be found alongside these other women, begetting life with no distinction of persons? Or are they still pleading to maintain their quality of 'set apart', seeking to symbolise something different through it? There is no one reply to these questions; there are as many and varied answers as there are people trying to express them and put them into practice. So all I can do here is shed some light on the interwoven strands of their history so as to unravel the original intention, buried under centuries of repetition of the same formulas.

It seems to me that, beyond the institutionalised character of religious life, beyond the clerical domination it has suffered, beyond the distortions and contradictions it has thrown up throughout its history, there is an 'intuition' in this 'institution'. The religious life did not set out to be an institution, but creative liturgy. And liturgy is the expression of a dream one would like to see fulfilled, or the memory of something marvellous that has filled one's life with meaning. The liturgy is 'rendering an account' that includes the possibility of the impossible, that mobilises the capacity to hope against hope, and to proclaim Life symbolically as the supreme value. Liturgy is not a copy of reality; it is the expression of a dream, of what we hope for and can never cease hoping for.

The liturgy of this dream set out to be a place where brotherhood, sharing, giving, relationships of love and justice—'paradise', in effect— could finally be put into practice as a way of life. And yet the intuition became the institution, the beautiful dream was turned into a reality based on rigid rules, and the liturgy disappeared. There is no way of legislating dreams; submitting them to rules means killing them in some way. And so the spell was broken. Virgins cannot be forced to give birth, breasts do not flow with milk to order, arms give no warmth unless their embrace comes from the heart. The Rule seems to have killed the dream, the cold letter of the law has replaced the spontaneity of love, solemnity has obscured beauty, fear of sin has paralysed energies. And once again the ghost called 'crisis' has appeared, a name that serves in a multitude of different situations.

Today, with some exceptions, we are experiencing nostalgia for the dream, for the original intuition, for the ability to make beautiful music whose melody we hear deep down in our bodies, but which we cannot flesh out with harmony. The flesh we have now seems to be rotting, our bones to be drying out, while we wait for the divine breath that will give new life in all its varied expressions: 'I shall put sinews in you and make flesh grow on you; I shall cover you with skin and give you my spirit, that you may live' (Ezek. 37:6).

It does not seem to me important to trace the causes that snuffed out the liturgy of the dream. Human history is complex and hard to unravel. What is certain is that it was the institutional Church, in its desire to keep the dream, that imprisoned it. It sought to control it, to make it uniform, clear and distinct, subject to the laws of reason and of Holy Mother Church. And now, is the dream over? Will no new collective dreams, new essays at a more human world, not emerge? Will women cease coming together, jointly to write a new Poetry that will touch human entrails and help us all to live?

I do not believe the dream is finished: dreaming is an essential part of the human condition. But, as Ecclesiastes says, 'there is a time for everything'. Now is the time in which the institution of 'spiritual motherhood' cannot dream. It is stunned by nightmares, worn out under the weight of its bureaucracy, its reports and conferences, all witnessing to its lack of ability to dream as an institution.

We have seen that true 'spiritual motherhood', the sort that really helps life to burst forth, has leaped over the walls of the institution and shown that the gift of begetting Life in the Spirit cannot be contained in prefabricated or carefully guarded models. These can continue to exist, and no doubt will do so, but unless I am much mistaken, it would seem that renewal of the face of the earth and life more abundant will not come from them. They will cling fearfully to certain traditions, in the belief that 'eternal values' reside in these. Therefore, they will resist novelty as though it were a threat to defined 'truths' which give security and stability.

It is quite possible that some people will be saddened by this time, seeing it as one in which Christian values and traditions are being lost. I would rather look on it as an 'intermezzo', a long interval, a hopeful period of waiting. Today, we can no longer try to restore forms of life that served well in other times. The basic intuition to go out to meet those who have 'fallen by the wayside', the need for dreams of solidarity and sharing, for liturgies of hope, for glimpses of the future, for the liturgy of the Greater Mystery: these are all demands made by our world of men and women.

We need patience to pick out the seeds bearing vital energy for today and tomorrow from the midst of the chaos—and the 'order'—in which we

live. Institutionalised 'spiritual motherhood' has to get into the swim with
this current of life, without trying to keep as its special privilege what the
Spirit has sown in different ways in men and women throughout history.
To die of old age as an institution is not the major problem, whatever
suffering and pain this may cause us as a body. Death and life go
hand in hand: we cannot have one without the other. The important thing
is to keep the lamps trimmed to the end, so as to hand them on to
those who will go on believing that Life is more than this or that way
of life.

4. Conclusion

Just a few brief words to conclude these thoughts, words of a
theologian-poet friend, words that seem to me full of hope, of that hope
that is being in love with humanity, that is motherhood, fatherhood,
gestation of the future:

I want to plant a tree. What sort, I don't yet know. Its canopy must be
broad, so that children can sit under it. And its branches should be
strong: I remember an old mango tree from my childhood, on which I
hung a swing. And I think of the sparrows that will come, when its fruit
is ripe. . . . But most important of all: it must grow slowly, very slowly.
It will have take so long to grow that I shan't live to sit in its shade. I
shall love it for the dreams that shelter in it.[6]

Translated by Paul Burns

Notes

1. I. Gebara, *As incômodas filhas de Eva* (São Paulo, NYP); R. Radford Reuther,
New Woman, New Earth (New York 1975).
2. R. Hostie, *Vie et mort des ordres religieux: approches psychosociologiques* (Paris
1972).
3. *Miroir spirituel de l'âme religieuse* (Paris 1898)—text for internal circulation in
the Congregation of Our Lady.
4. *Op. cit.*, p. 57.
5. M. J. Rosado Nunes, *Vida religiosa nos meios populares* (Petrópolis 1985).
6. R. Alves, *Pai Nosso, Meditações* (São Paulo 1987), p. 82.

PART II

The Ethics and Politics of Motherhood

Christine Gudorf

Women's Choice for Motherhood: Beginning a Cross-cultural Approach

AS A comprehensive cross-cultural approach to women's choice for motherhood is impossible within the limits of a single article, I will focus on three types of overt restrictions on women's choice for motherhood: forbidding women choice about marriage, refusing women choice about sexual intercourse within and outside marriage, and social coercion in or absence of birth control and child care. Most societies are experiencing changes in one or more of these areas today.

In Islamic societies, which hold 17 per cent of the world's population, the greatest tensions between modernisation and Islamic law in this century have centred on women and the family, especially (1) restricting/forbidding polygamy (as in Turkey and Tunisia)[1] and child marriage, both allowed under traditional Islamic law, and (2) granting greater rights to women, as in rejection of the veil and access to divorce.[2] Early marriage contracted by fathers to a groom sometimes unseen until the ceremony, and difficult access to contraception, sterilisation and abortion are frequently still the rule in Islamic societies though poor women, as everywhere in developing nations, are often pressured to undergo sterilisation or use contraception by government programmes for development. Since the modesty, obedience to husbands, and fertility urged of women in the Quran are considered obligatory,[3] the idea that women have choices about marital intercourse is inconceivable; rape is by definition limited to non-marital situations. Sex outside marriage can have consequences under religious and civil law as serious as lifetime seclusion.[4] The majority of women do not work outside the home, child care is virtually restricted to informal arrangements, and women provide virtually all child care.

In the Soviet Union patterns of life differ greatly between European (Russian, Belorussian, Georgian, Balt and Ukrainian) women and non-European women, especially the Moslems of the Central Asian Republics. Soviet women have been much more influenced by decades of government policy aimed at emancipating women (in male-defined terms) through participation in production.[5] Women make up 51 per cent of the workforce (53 per cent of the population),[6] and housework and childcare, which early communist policy promised to socialise, remains almost exclusively the task of these working women, whose average workload is therefore 15–20 per cent higher than men's.[7] This has impacted birthrates to the point that today the government encourages Soviet women to have more children, lest the higher birthrates among the non-Soviets lead to a majority from the more backward areas. Today Soviet birthrates hover between 3.1 and 3.3 per cent, by comparison, in Tadzhikistan the birthrate is 6.6 per cent with 26.1 per cent of married women having seven children or more. Non-Soviet women also marry younger, often by parental choice, and seldom work outside the home.

Contraception, like consumer goods in general, is difficult to obtain throughout the USSR, especially outside the cities, but legal abortion is available for a very low fee, and constitutes the major form of birth control.[8] In order to control family size, Soviet women are willing to undergo several abortions, despite unsympathetic staff at clinics and the absence or inadequate use of anaesthetics. The government pays 50 roubles to a mother for a first child, and 100 roubles for a second or third, and gives priority in housing lists to newlyweds and couples with children.[9]

In Africa, there are great varieties between cultures in choices allowed women. One practice found in East, West, and Central Africa, the Islamic countries of the Middle East, Africa and Asia, and in Brazil, eastern Mexico, Peru and among the Australian aborigines, is genital mutilation of women. Clitorectomy is practiced in Syria by rubbing ground pepper onto the clitoris of newborn girls until it disappears.[10] Among the Kenyan Nandi, female puberty rites begin at 10 for girls, who are made to sleep with boys without sex, then checked for virginity, the loss of which occasionally results in the girl being speared to death. At about 14, girls' clitorises are surgically removed by older women after ceremonial dances to celebrate their coming of age.[11] In Sierra Leone women's societies organise great ceremonies around clitorectomies for girls.[12] Among the Maasai and the Akamba of East Africa female puberty ritual involves excising part of the clitoris. (Among Maasai boys, the age mates who are circumcised together in puberty rituals become so bonded that wives are interchangeable.[13]) In Sudan, to call a girl *ghalfa* (one who retains the clitorial hood) insults her marriagability.[14] Genital infibulation, the removal of the clitoris, labia minora, and most of the labia majora, with the remains stitched together, leaving only small openings for urine and menstrual flow, occurs in some African nations.[15] Clitorectomy satisfies norms for marriagability and is believed to protect men from dangerous clitorial contact, and, by removing female orgasmic capacity, to ensure virginity before marriage and fidelity after marriage. Genital infibulation makes each act of intercourse 'virginal', that is tissue-tearing and tight, to enhance male pleasure. In polygamous cultures the more severe forms of genital mutilation serve to promote bonding between women in the household rather than with the spouse. There are about 30 million living women who have undergone genital mutilation.[16]

In many regions of Africa, rural women often carry on subsistence agriculture, raising children more or less alone, while men migrate to cities for work. South African apartheid, which considers Africans natives of the barren 'Homelands' where there is no work, requires African workers who migrate to the cities for work to leave their families behind. Evidence in Africa suggests that nutritional deficiency in mothers stunts their growth which, in turn, causes significant maternal risk in childbirth. Mother and child health programmes focus on child health, ignoring mothers.[17] In some African societies, difficulties in labour are considered evidence of adultery requiring confession.[18]

Many developing societies have been introduced to modern contraception through development programmes; unfortunately, women gain little choice. Indonesia, for example, has a 'successful' record in achieving the widespread use of contraception by means of a two-step process: (1) enlisting descending levels of male hierarchy to the village level to use their authority in coercing those under them to accept contraception, and (2) rewarding complying households with credit, training, and public awards.[19] Kenya's failed contraception programme came to be popularly understood as motivated by white demographic interests and not concern for women's and children's health. Using the pill, the Kenyan programme required a medical infrastructure the nation did not have. Kenyan women would probably accept non-coercive contraception integrated with supporting mother and infant health programmes, since poor rural women struggle, amid high infant mortality and obstetrical complications, to feed their children by subsistence agriculture, while many men migrate for work.

In Latin America women generally choose whether and whom to marry, though arranged marriage occasionally persists among indigenous peoples.

Women are seen as made to be mothers, and are respected largely for motherhood. Youth often use pregnancy to force parental consent to marriage despite Church condemnation of pre-marital sex. Men frequently beat wives, especially when drunk, and defend this practice publicly.[20] Women have little choice over marital sex. Abortion is prohibited in two-thirds of the Latin American nations though illegal abortion causes over 20 per cent of maternal deaths in those nations where it is illegal.[21] Sterilisation is outlawed in Latin American nations such as Peru, though Colombia hosts one of the world's most vigorous sterilisation drives, and El Salvador is the scene of another push. In Brazil, where sterilisation is also illegal, women often undergo unnecessary caesarean sections in order to obtain a discreet tubectomy.

Temporary means of contraception are permitted and even provided to the poor at low or no cost in most Latin American nations. Such provision, however, is frequently, as elsewhere, linked to 'incentives' and 'disincentives' both to poor women and to officials who fill high quotas of women sterilised or provided with IUDs or pills. Many women are not provided with follow-up care; they suffer side effects from the pill and IUDs without medical redress. Others report never being told sterilisation was permanent.

In Peru the fertility rate is 4.6 children per woman; 80 per cent of women of childbearing age in sexual unions do not want another pregnancy; 60 per cent of women over 35 with three children or more did not want their last pregnancy. Twenty per cent of women are beaten by their husbands or live-in partners. Forty-one per cent of women in sexual unions use contraception; of these 24 per cent use traditional methods (rhythm, douching, herbs, withdrawal) and 17 per cent modern methods. Peru is the only nation in Latin America, and Peru, Haiti, Mauritanius, Philippines, South Korea and Sri Lanka are the only nations in the world, where 5 per cent or more of the population uses rhythm, despite its being the only contraceptive method approved by the Church.[22] During 1988 Peruvian bishops successfully killed a bill passed in the lower house allowing women with three children or more and spousal consent to choose sterilisation. Peruvian law requires employers to grant paid maternity leave to women; but, as in many developing nations, most employed women work in the informal sector, without employers.

Among the poor in Latin America, as elsewhere, women report opposition by sexual partners to the use of contraceptives. Male opposition is strongest where women (not men) provide the bulk of support for children; men deprived of pride as providers are loath to forgo another traditional method for demonstrating masculinity. Lack of work is a chief cause of a major social problem: men's abandonment of women and children.

Between 1981 and 1984 the maternal death rate in Peru was 314 per 100,000 births, compared to 55 in Chile, and 33 in Cuba, but 5 in Holland and 4 in Switzerland. In Peru, less than 22 per cent of pregnant women receive pre-natal care, 70 per cent of children are both without medical attention, and 33.3 per cent of pregnant women suffer nutritional anemia.[23] Infant mortality varies widely between rural and urban areas; Peru's overall rate is 88 per 1000, but the rate in rural Andean departments soars to over 270 per 1000.

In China since the comprehensive Marriage Law of 1950, there is no arranged marriage, and women have the right to divorce.[24] The right of wives to refuse sex is unclear. Sex outside of marriage is severely discouraged, especially non-contraceptive non-marital sex. The most controversial aspect of motherhood in China today is the birth limitation policy. Through strong pressure to delay marriage, to use contraception and to abort, the government attempts to limit births to one child per family. One-child families have free child care, medical care and education, privileged access to housing, private farm plots, and adult grain rations for the child; families with two lose these, and suffer other discrimination.

There have been many cases of compulsory abortion, even in the last trimester, especially of third children.[25] Infanticide, even of first children if female, has risen sharply. During the 1979–81 introduction of the new policy, the percentage of girl infants dropped from 48.4 per cent to 41.8 per cent. Since 1984 there is more laxity in rural areas where opposition was strongest; now two children are often allowed farm families. Remarried couples are allowed a child even if parents by previous marriage; sometimes a second child is allowed if the first was a girl, or handicapped. Little research on male-female workloads exists, though many women work outside the home. Child care exists, but child care and housework in the home remain the woman's obligation.

Among Hindus of India and Bangladesh, little choice exists for women regarding motherhood. Arranged marriage and multiple children by age twenty are still common. The influence of traditional religious codes of ethics, such as *Manu*, which stipulated that wives be obedient and faithful even if husbands are deformed, unfaithful, drunken, debauched, and abusive, remains strong.[26] Women have few rights within marriage, especially in sex. In the Himalayas, a wife is considered sexually available at all time to her husband and his brothers.[27] Bearing sons is women's primary means of gaining status and respect. Mothers-in-law, not wives, rule the household. In India in recent years there have been newspaper accounts of husbands and mother-in-laws killing wives to obtain a second wife's dowry.

Both India and Bangladesh have a record of massive abuses in coerced sterilisation of the poor. In India, round-ups of men—in a few cases all the village men—by police and military for compulsory vasectomy brought down Indira Gandhi's government in 1977. Coerced sterilisation continues to be common, though government policy after 1978 shifted to female sterilisation as less politically volatile. Now 80 per cent of sterilisations are by tubectomy, a much riskier operation than vasectomy. 70 per cent of sterilisations are performed in camps, under appalling unsterile conditions, with little or no followup. Only the elite are given the choice of the IUD; the poor are considered too ignorant to cope with anything but sterilisation. Payment for sterilisation is $22 for women and $15 for men.

In 1983 the Bangladeshi army launched a campaign of compulsory sterilisation in the north, and in a few weeks rounded up and sterilised over 500 poor women against their will.[28] In the wake of the devastating floods of 1984, women were offered relief food only if sterilised, whether young and childless or not. Sterilisations rose precipitously during the flood months: July–October 1984 saw 257,000, 25 per cent of the entire 1972–1982 decade's total. Thirty-four per cent of contraceptive users in Bangladesh are sterilised; the government intends to raise this to 41 per cent by 1990.[29] Each person sterilised received 175 *taka* (several weeks wages) and a new sari. Sterilisations rise dramatically during the lean autumn months before the rice harvest. Reviewers of sterilisation programmes find a shocking lack of hygeine in the centres, and a failure of 40 per cent of the centres to adequately inform patients about the permanency of the surgery. One report followed 950 sterilised persons: it took more than a third of the women 45 days or more to return to work, and 80 per cent had to seek some form of medical treatment after surgery, for which they had to pay. One third of the women said sterilisation was the only method of contraception of which they had been informed.

In the United States, and the developed world in general, women decide when and if to marry, and whether to have intercourse outside marriage. Within marriage, many women do not have that right; only half the states in the United States recognise the possibility of rape in marriage. The United States has one of the highest incidences of rape in the world; at present rates 25 per cent of women are raped during their lifetime.[30] Access to contraception and abortion depend upon individual economic circumstances. Abortion is legal, regulated, and relatively expensive. All forms of contraception tested and approved by the government's Food and Drug Administration are available, though some drugs available in Europe (*e.g.* RU 486) face long approval processes. Medical insurance for welfare recipients does not cover abortion, though it covers 90 per cent of sterilisation costs and virtually all expenses for other types of contraception. The poor who do not qualify for welfare programmes often cannot afford many kinds of contraception; in the USA efficient, cost-effective contraceptives require either a prescription or a fitting/insertion (for diaphram, cervical cap, or IUD) necessitating a physician's fee.

Over half the women in the USA work outside the home, most for economic reasons. The USA, unlike other developed nations such as France, Sweden, Hungary, East and West Germany, does not guarantee paid maternity leave or family income support for child rearing.[31] These other nations have extensive state supported child care; the USA has only private child care, which, without government subsidy, is expensive. Half USA marriages end in divorce, with women usually receiving custody of children. Divorce most commonly impoverishes women; over two-thirds of mothers of children with absent fathers receive either no child support or less than the stipulated amount.[32] Because fathers do little childcare or housework, working wives average 76 hours work per week, while their husbands average between 40.3 and 42.7 hours per week.[33]

Poor black and Hispanic women in the USA are frequently offered consent forms for sterilisation during hospital delivery, and sterilised by means of hysterectomies, a procedure 15–20 times more dangerous than tubectomy. This practice has been defended as a demographic necessity which gives surgical practice to interns and residents in general hospitals. In 1976 the US General Accounting Office revealed that the federally funded Indian Health Service had sterilised 3000 Native American women in four years using consent forms 'not in compliance' with regulations.[34]

Our world is far from meeting even minimum conditions for an ethic of motherhood. Women are given and taken in marriage, seized for rape and battery, mutilated and sterilised as matters of policy, and assigned more work than men. Minimum criteria for an ethic of motherhood must include: (1) respect for women's rights to make decisions in their lives: on marriage, sex, work, and contraception; (2) the opening of female roles to alternatives including but not requiring motherhood and child care; (3) respect for women, their bodies, their control of their bodies and for sexual interaction as mutuality not domination; (4) acceptance by men of equal responsibility for child care, housework, and financial support of children; (5) social support for parenting: paid maternity leave and affordable quality daycare; (6) open, non-coercive access for all women to a variety of safe, effective means of contraception; (7) social support for lowering and equalising maternal and infant mortality rates by addressing poverty which afflicts women and children most.

Notes

1. Jane I. Smith, 'Islam', in *Women and World Religions*, ed. Arvind Sharma (Albany 1987), p. 237.
2. John J. Donohue and John L. Esposito, eds., *Islam in Transition: Muslim Perspectives* (New York 1982), p. 200.
3. Denise L. Carmody, *Women and World Religions* (Englewood Cliffs 1989), p. 196.
4. *Ibid.*, p. 192.
5. Marilyn Rueshmeyer, *Professional Work and Marriage: An East-West Comparison* (Hong Kong 1981), p. 116.
6. Jo Peers, 'Workers by Hand and Womb—Soviet Women and the Demographic Crisis', in *Soviet Sisterhood*, ed. Barbara Holland (Bloomington, IN 1985), p. 117.
7. Maggie McAndrew, 'Soviet Women's Magazines', in *Soviet Sisterhood*, p. 112.
8. *Op. cit.*, p. 134.
9. Mary Buckley, 'Soviet Interpretations of the Woman Question', in *Soviet Sisterhood*, p. 48.
10. W. Ohm, 'Female Circumcision', *Sexology Today* (June 1980), pp. 21–25.
11. John Mbiti, *African Religions and Philosophy* (New York 1969), pp. 166–171.
12. Carmody, pp. 29–30.
13. *Op. cit.*, pp. 159–166.
14. Robert Crooks and Karla Baur, *Our Sexuality* (Indianapolis 1983), p. 660.
15. R. H. O. Banerman, 'Integrating Traditional and Modern Health Systems', *Advances in Maternal and Child Health*, Vol. 2, ed. D. B. Jelliffe and E. F. P. Jelliffe (Oxford 1982), p. 38.
16. C. Brisset, 'Female Mutilation: Cautious Forum on Damaging Practices', *The Guardian*, 18 March 1979.
17. Deborah Howard, 'Aspects of Maternal Morbidity: The Experience of Less Developed Countries', *Advances in Maternal and Child Health*, Vol. 7, ed. D. B. Jelliffe and E. F. P. Jelliffe (Oxford 1987), p. 2.
18. *Ibid.*, p. 4.
19. Betsy Hartman, *Reproductive Rights and Wrongs: The Global Politics of Population Control and Reproductive Choice* (New York 1987), pp. 74–83.
20. Lourdes Arizpe and Josefina Aranda, 'Women Workers in the Strawberry Agribusiness in Mexico', in *Women's Work*, eds. Eleanor Leacock and Helen I. Safa (South Hadley, MA 1986), p. 185.
21. *Op. cit.*, p. 245.
22. El Movimiento Feminista, '¿Mortalidad Materna Es Evitable?', pamphlet for Dia Internacional de Acción por la salud de la Mujer, 28 de mayo de 1988, p. 6.
23. *Ibid.*, pp. 5–8.
24. Carmody, p. 112.
25. Hartman, p. 152.
26. *Op. cit.*, p. 51.
27. Gerald D. Berreman, *Hindus of the Himalayas* (Berkeley 1974), pp. 171–172.

28. Hartman, p. 217.
29. *Ibid.*, p. 214.
30. Mary Pellauer, 'Moral Callousness and Moral Sensitivity', in *Women's Consciousness, Women's Conscience* eds. Barbara Andolsen, Christine Gudorf and Mary Pellauer (New York 1987), pp. 38–39.
31. Sheila B. Kamerman and Alfred J. Kahn, *Child Care, Family Benefits, and Working Parents: A Study in Comparative Policy* (New York 1981).
32. Andrew Cherlin, *Marriage, Divorce, Remarriage* (Cambridge, MA 1983), pp. 87–88.
33. Barbara Andolsen, 'A Woman's Work is Never Done', in *Women's Consciousness*, p. 5.
34. Hartman, pp. 240–241.

Johanna Kohn-Roelin

Mother—Daughter—God

Traversing the generations from grandmother to mother to daughter is a particular psychology which has its roots and its flesh in the experience of being female in a patriarchal culture.[1]

Eva Gottschald remembers:

We meet God through our mother and both—mother and God—are frightening, incomprehensible ... Nothing can be hidden from our parents or God. They make children tell them what they want to know. HE sees everything, even when you are completely alone. It gives you the creeps ... Sexuality is not something to be enjoyed but a very serious matter ... I find it painful when I undress at night and my mother watches me and discusses the changes happening to my body in puberty with my father ... Religious upbringing and mother upbringing. Fear of God. Fear of the mother. You can't set boundaries between them.[2]

1. Parent-God and child-creature

SINCE THE publication of Tilman Moser's *Gottesvergiftung*[3] many autobiographical writers—both female and male—have attested the connection between the masculine image of God in an expressly authoritarian religion and the sufferings of generations of women and men inflicted by a rigid super-ego.

Feminist criticism from M. Daly onwards has systematically explored this connection between psychology and theology. It has explored the role of masculine language about God in maintaining male domination and the patriarchal oppression of women. It rediscovered female images of God in the Christian biblical and post-biblical tradition, which enabled women to rediscover themselves as images of God and develop a new theological self-awareness.

But, as our second quote above reminds us, the mother as 'Mother God'[4] can also have authoritarian and patriarchal features, which can hinder the daughter's emancipation and damage her identity and personal integrity. In order to consider which female images of God are truly liberating rather than oppressive, we must look at the social and psycho-social conditions and relationships women grow up in today.

In our first quotation psychotherapists Orbach and Eichenbaum spoke about the mother—daughter relationship. Here patriarchy is seen as not just external oppression but internal self-oppression, passed on from generation to generation. Women's upbringing for motherhood means they are brought up as second-class human beings.

2. The mother's powerless power

There is a contradiction between the high value placed upon motherliness and motherhood by Church and society and the actual position they grant to women who are mothers. The idealisation of the mother in looking after her children, her capacity to give birth, her care of the disadvantaged and deep religious feeling is an astonishingly new phenomenon. It arose with the nineteenth-century relegation of religion and love of neighbour to the private sphere of the bourgeois family. H. Häring notes the paradox that 'the rediscovery of the feminine in religious symbolism in the nineteenth century goes hand in hand with the withdrawal from the public domain'.[5] The home is the bourgeois woman's sphere. The husband and father becomes increasingly absent from the family. His absence means that 'the mother, whose relegation to the smaller family has made her socially powerless, becomes psychically over-dominant within it.'[6] She prepares the children for their social function in the 'outside world',—according to their specific gender roles, of course.[7] The boy is brought up to be someone different from the mother and to go out into the world. For the girl the mother is the model for her own future. Religion and society acknowledge the mother in her capacity to be clever, beautiful, good, pious and strong for others, and her pride in giving birth. The daughter absorbs both this acknowledgment and her mother's experience that its price is high. For example, motherhood often makes it difficult to find a job. If a woman decides not to become a mother, she faces social and moral disapproval unless her decision goes hand in hand with sexual abstinence or she leads a life of 'spiritual motherhood' for others.

The latest encyclical *Mulieries dignitatem* tells us that women who become mothers are linked to God's covenant with the human race through the motherhood of God's mother.[8] Accordingly women's mission is to hand on the love they have received. God entrusts humanity to women in a special way—meaning the service of motherhood.[9] But this does not mean that women are offered any correspondingly important liturgical service or ordination to the ministries of the Church.

The bourgeois and religious ideal of motherhood is against working women, lesbians and unmarried women. It is also against women who by a sort of heroic juggling act try to combine motherhood with a job. Hostility to women is expressed in the official view of 'motherliness' itself. This naive idealisation also occurs when so-called positive feminine attributes are recommended as a way of preventing the catastrophes at present threatening us, which are usually produced by men—women as 'global housewives' and 'moppers up'.[10]

However we find that this ideal image of motherhood does not give women any corresponding power in society. Even when feminine images are used to symbolise the divine, paradoxically these images convey something highly valued but subordinate. Motherhood and motherliness are not attributes women have among others, but their only acceptable ones. Publicly the ideal of 'being a mother' is loaded with sentiment, whereas in reality society exploits mothers. We cannot discuss motherhood only in religious terms. At least feminist reflection must take reality into account, and feminist theology must also question femininity as motherhood. This concerns all women, whether they are mothers or not. Every woman is a mother's daughter.

3. On femininity as motherliness

The mother—daughter relationship is crucial to the formation of the feminine psyche. Largely in agreement with N. Chodorow,[11] the psychotherapists S. Orbach and L. Eichenbaum describe the development of femininity as socialisation for motherliness and motherhood. Here are some aspects of this development:

4. Identification

The foundations of femininity are laid in the daughter's early years.

Because she is the same sex, the mother becomes a model for her daughter. The daughter identifies with the mother and thus learns about her own sex and gender role. And the mother also re-experiences herself in the daughter. She remembers her own hopes, fears and experiences as a girl and these flow into her relationship with her daughter. Because the mother knows what it means to be a girl, she communicates to the daughter her joy and pride in motherhood as well as her feeling of being uncared for, her unsatisfied longing for nurturing, her fear of her own needs for sex, power and dependency. As a little girl the mother learnt to conceal this side of herself, so she will find it difficult to cope when her daughter expresses spontaneous sexual and emotional needs.

5. Defence

The mother—daughter relationship is governed by the ambivalence felt by the mother between symbiotic closeness and defence, *i.e.* punishment of the daughter's own activities. The girl comes to feel that she has a good acceptable side and a bad side, which must be hidden and rejected. This side goes underground and lives on as the so-called 'little girl' in the grown woman.

6. Being a mother means living for

The daughter thus has a huge double programme to undertake in her psychic development: she learns to restrict her own activities but must also learn to be emotionally independent. She is brought up to please her father and husband without expecting emotional satisfaction from it. The 'construction of femininity' only succeeds when she has learnt 'to give what others need; and she gives to others out of the well of her own unmet needs'.[12] But the mother also brings her own unmet needs into the relationship with the daughter—even though, as N. Chodorow points out, these really belong in a relationship between adults. The daughter responds to these needs by trying to take care of the mother. Thus the mother becomes the daughter's first child.

Thou shalt not be separate is the secret commandment the mother gives her daughter. But even if the daughter obeys this command, she does not experience the promised closeness. In this ambivalent relationship the mother has enormous power. She cares for and punishes, comforts and hurts, embraces and repels. But the daughter can only achieve individuation, develop into a personality, a self with firm boundaries and self awareness if the break from the mother is made successfully.[13]

7. The drama of the feminist daughter

Other factors besides the new generation's striving for autonomy affect the process of breaking free from the mother. In discussion with M. S. Mahler, E. Jacobson and A. Freud, E. Reinke declares 'the mother who resists or hinders the development of the child's self aggravates the conflict in the child between striving for autonomy and the ongoing persistent desire for dependency. This quite often leads to the development of a pseudo-autonomy and a kind of counter-identity.'[14]

Her thesis is harsh but worthy of attention. It holds that the kind of feminism in which women not only resort to women-only groups as a way of working out their problems but place *all* hopes of liberation in the emancipation of women and the development of womanpower bears signs of this false autonomy and counter-identity. The pairing of house and housewifely, mother and motherly, man and manly is regarded as 'irrational', a mere negative mythology. But it is this very striving to prove that you are different from your mother and better than male colleagues, which betrays a counter-dependency on the myth. The feminist movement increases women's self confidence and powers of performance but the longterm demands it makes on the self show that it is clearly a new form of the old dependency: performance is not 'for its own sake' but for approval (by the father?/the all-powerful mother?)

This approval-seeking means that women continue to be exploitable by society and at work. The new form of exploitation may be expressed in the expectation that women with their womanliness and motherliness should undertake the job of humanising both private and public life.

Isn't it now time that women should refuse to carry this whole burden alone? Shouldn't we demand that men in full awareness of their limitation should also play their part in working for liberation and a more just, non-sexist society?

Women can renounce their fantasies of omnipotence. This means positively that they can be freed from the pressure to live up to false ideals. Fully aware of their own limitations and needs, women can then say: it is enough to be a woman. A woman does not have to prove herself by her feminism. Her demands for changes in political and personal life, at home and at work, need her thought and energy. They do not need justification.

8. New mothers? New fathers?

But the theory and practice of the 'new mother' and 'new father' often goes against this.

Fathers who try to be the best mothers and mothers who replace the father may compete for symbiotic closeness with their children. Then we get what J. Bopp and E. Reinke have critically dubbed the 'super-mother' and the 'nursing father'.[15] They consider that both these forms of parenthood hinder the children's individuation. The parents helplessly often oppose their children's wishes for autonomy with aggression and fear.[16] Both the mother and the father fail to realise the importance of the father with his masculinity in the child's necessary separation process. If the father is lacking, either because he 'mothers', because he is really absent, or because the mother regards him as dangerous or unimportant, and the parents fear their children's separation from them, the child may become 'estranged'. The parents' behaviour cause the child to feel separation anxiety and this dampens curiosity about what is new and different. M. S Mahler did a series of investigations establishing that it is the father who is important to the daughter at this stage in her life, because he represents the other and the new. He can increase her self-confidence and make her emancipation less difficult. Therefore, says E. Reinke, we must 'restore the split-off masculine into the emancipation process. Not just the adolescent's emancipation from parents. It is also necessary in the women's movement itself. Otherwise the movement will lose its emancipatory power through a new myth, which makes the ONE an absolute and splits off the OTHER.' U. Pfäfflin describes some possible consequences:

Girls will benefit from their father's emotional closeness and steadiness. Painful experiences and separations will become more bearable. Not all the negative experiences in the child's psychic structure will be centred on the mother, everything bad will not derive from disappointments with women. Moreover not all progress will be ascribed to the thought, energy and work of men.

This would mean an end to women's self-destruction; up till now they have been accomplices in their own silencing and the repression of their powers. If they stop hating their mothers and themselves, they will have a chance to stop the suicidal swing between over-expectation and undervaluing. They themselves, their children and their partners will have the space to blossom and enjoy their lives.[17]

9. Language about God and women's socialisation

Theology is concerned with the socialisation of women because it is concerned with how to speak about God. We start with the fact that, as J. B. Metz says, speaking about God can no longer be done at the expense of speaking about humans. According to the doctrine of analogy, all language about God and specific images of God are always more unlike than like God.[18] Images of God always give more information about the speakers, their needs, fears, hopes, political and social relations, than about God, who remains a mystery.

One way in the which the Bible expresses this mystery is in the prohibition of idol worship and graven images. But this does not mean that it does not matter which analogous images stand for God and which stories symbolise the relationship between God and humanity. Though the New Testament scriptures portray God as the loving Father of Jesus Christ, the scriptures of the Jewish tradition confess HIM/HER as just and liberating, faithful and strong. But the message of salvation, which, as J. B. Metz puts it, calls all human beings living and dead to become persons in his sight, is not 'pure'. It is always conveyed through scriptural witnesses, mainly male authors, and always experienced in behaviour between human beings. Religious socialisation must become a way for faith to support interpersonal behaviour which makes for solidarity and the achievement of identity. Autobiographical accounts by many women, and men too in a different way, tell us about psychic illness and damage to the process of achieving personal identity, not just religious identity. If religious socialisation is responsible for such illnesses and damage, they threaten the faith's credibility and are a stumbling block to its preaching.

All theology, not just feminist theology, must therefore take responsibility for language about God which can cope with 'all the pressures that psychically deform women and make them socially second-class beings'.[19] Thus theology's aim must be more than the re-interpretation of Christian tradition, salvaging biblical and post-biblical women's history, and for example, reclaiming female names of God. Its goal must be to change reality for both men and women, so that their lives enable them to achieve their own identity, free from all forms of oppression, sexism, racism or anti-semitism.

10. Mother God: mother or God?

There is a obvious relationship between childhood experience, religious symbols and the life that follows. In the so-called detachment and individuation stage of early childhood, the decisive positive and negative experiences with the mother and father are carried over into the child's image of God, if the parents make God and his word part of the relationship.[20] The child's image of God will use real experiences with the mother and also hopes and wishes about her. So the child's image of God is always partly projection. As A. Miller and P. Schellbaum[21] put it, if there are traumatic experiences with the parents, these can be carried over metaphysically into the image of God. The opening quote from E. Gottschaldt makes the same point. On the other hand a happy relationship between mother and daughter may also become a symbol for a God who takes care of you and fundamentally accepts you.

Images of God do not only derive from the mother-child and parent-child relationship. They are also come from the Church and its institutions. Liberating language about God can be really effective. Psychology of religion shows how the images of God contains real parental male and female characteristics and real childhood experiences of suffering. It can therefore help a client achieve a greater awareness and restore their power to act positively because it will help them see which parts of the experienced suffering can be worked on, where their personal situation can be changed and where it must sadly be accepted. Theology must show in faith that its language about God is a message of salvation to all human beings; it must ensure that this language also adequately expresses women's likeness to God.

Feminist theology knows that God must also be expressed in female symbols, so that women can identify with them. Girls need to recognise themselves in language about God. It matters that God should be represented as a woman kneading bread (Luke 13:18), as a mother bird (Ps. 17:8) as a woman giving birth (Deut. 32:18), as a woman in labour (Isa. 66:9), and a comforting mother (Isa. 66:13). Thus women can experience themselves and recognise themselves as God's images. Girls' religious experience will be influenced in this way very strongly. And of course they will also be influenced by stories of women in the Bible, Ruth, Miriam, Mary Magdalene and others, if they are brought up with them. Their religious self-awareness will also depend on how well mothers and daughters succeed in holding on to these female forms, even through the androcentric distortion of the story-tellers. Among other things, the future of theology will depend on whether it takes notice of particular damaged and limited mothers and daughters, who live in particular social, cultural, religious and private relationships and speaks about them in a new way.

Translated by Dinah Livingstone

Notes

1. L. Eichenbaum and S. Orbach, *Understanding Women* (Harmondsworth 1985), p. 38.

2. E. Gottschald, 'Muttergott' in D. Scherf (ed.), *Der liebe Gott sieht alles* (Frankfurt 1986), pp. 54, 55, 57, 64.
3. T. Moser, *Gottesvergiftung* (Reinbeck 1976).
4. E. Gottschaldt, *op. cit.*, p. 54.
5. H. Häring, 'Die Mutter als schmerzensreiche. Zur Geschichte des Weiblichen in der Trinität' in M.-Th. Wacker (ed.), *Der Gott der Männer und die Frauen* (Düsseldorf 1987), p. 64.
6. U. Pfäfflin 'Muttermord-Spekulationen über die Macht von Müttern' in Pfäfflin and U. Passero (eds.), *Neue Mütterlichkeit* (Gütersloh 1986).
7. On the bringing up of children for gender-specific roles and theories thereon, see in particular: H. Bilden, 'Geschlechtsspezifische Sozialisation' in K. Hurrlemann and D. Ulich (eds.), *Handbuch der Sozialisationsforschung* (Weinheim, Basel 1980).
8. German Bishops' Conference Secretariat (ed.), *Apostolisches Schreiben Mulieris Dignitatem von Johannes Paul II. Uber die Würde und Berufung der Frau anlässlich des Marianischen Jahres* (Bonn 1988), p. 45.
9. *Op. cit.*, p. 66.
10. Ch. Thürmer-Rohr, 'Feminisierung der Gesellschaft. Weiblichkeit als Putz und Entseuchungsmittel', *ibid.* (ed.), *Vagabundinnen* (Berlin 1987), p. 106. *Cf.* also pp. 106ff.
11. *Cf.* N. Chodorow, *The Reproduction of Mothering* (1978).
12. L. Eichenbaum and S. Orbach, *op. cit.*, p. 56.
13. Cf. H. J. Fraas, 'Entwicklung und religiöse Sozialisation, in W. Böckrer, H. G. Heimbrock and E. Kerkhoff (eds.), *Handbuch religiöser Erziehung*, vol. 1 (Düsseldorf 1987), pp. 110ff.
14. E. Reinke, 'Das Eine ohne das Andere. Kann die Identitätsbildung und Autonomieentwicklung der Töchter sich Übermüttern verdanken? Plädoyer für die Wiederanerkennung des Vaters in der Identitätsbildung der Frau', J. Conrad and U. Konnertz (eds.), *Weiblichkeit in der Moderne* (Tübingen 1986), pp. 97f.
15. J. Bopp, 'Die Abschaffung der Vaterrolle, in S. R. Dunde (ed.), *Neue Väterlichkeit* (Gütersloh 1986), p. 86.
16. *Op. cit.*, p. 55.
17. U. Pfäfflin, *op. cit.*, p. 48.
18 Cf. H. Denziger and A. Schönmetzer, *Enchiridion symbolorum, definitioneum et declarationum de rebus fidei et morum* (Barcelona 1973), no. 806.
19. Th. Wacker, 'Feministische Theologie, in P. Eicher (ed.), *Neues Handbuch theologischer Grundbegriffe* (Munich 1984), p. 354.
20. *Cf.* H. J. Frass, *op. cit.*, p. 111.
21. **Cf.** A. Miller *Du sollst nicht merken* (Frankfurt 1983), P. Schellenbaum *Stichwort: Gottesbild* (Berlin 1981).

Dorry de Beijer

Motherhood and the New Forms of Reproductive Technology: Passive Source of Nutrition and Rational Consumer

WHAT CONTRIBUTION can a feminist ethic make to the discussions that have opened up both at international and local level about the new forms of reproductive technology, surrogate motherhood and genetic manipulation?

In the feminist literature of theology and ethics about this theme, which, to me, does not seem to be very extensive as yet, two tasks are put forward. The Swiss ethicist Ina Praetorius believes it important to question the ecclesiastical discussions and the medical-ethical and theological opinions. The North American theologian Margaret Farley places the emphasis elsewhere. She discusses moral issues that arise directly from the application of a certain technique: Is *in vitro* fertilisation acceptable from a feminist-theological perspective? What is the situation with women's moral autonomy during the treatment? What is the child's interest? She places these issues within a wider ethical domain: in what direction should reproductive technology be developed so that it can be applied in a humane and dignified way worldwide? This question suggests a third task for a feminist ethic: a critical examination of the technology itself.

In this article I aim to demonstrate that this critical examination is necessary in order to develop and expand an adequate feminist ethic of reproduction. I will do this by discussing an important issue within the current feminist discussions: the relation between individual freedom of choice, power, and technology. The changing feminist views on this affect

73

the central question and tasks of a feminist ethic. I will provide a beginning
for an ethic study of the technology. My questions will be: how much is
this technology based on patriarchal viewpoint, what meanings are given
to motherhood within that context, and what consequences can it have for
women?

At this juncture it is necessary to point out that my observations and
hypotheses are set within the context of the actual society of which I am
part, and within the discussions held by the Dutch movement, of which
mostly white women partake. These discussions are similar to those held in
West Germany and the United States, but have their own emphases on
moral issues regarding fertilisation techniques, pre-natal diagnosis, and
selective abortion in relation to hereditary 'abnormalities'. Issues on sex
selection techniques and surrogate motherhood receive less attention since
these are illegal in the Netherlands. Critical analysis of my own Western
context will hopefully serve as a first step towards a feminist approach to
a global problem that takes both the international political powers and the
common interest of women worldwide very seriously indeed.

1. Medical-technological control of reproduction

Feminists base the usage of the 'old' forms of reproductive technology—
contraception, sterilisation and abortion—on womens' right to make
choices about motherhood and reproduction. To Western feminists this
means above all the right to have access to the techniques and to be able to
postpone motherhood. This 'pro choice' claim radically opposes the
patriarchal ideology which regards motherhood as a woman's true aim in
life. Feminist theologians B. Wildung Harrison and C. Heyward stress that
the right of freedom of choice is not a liberal one but implies a re-balancing
of the power between the sexes. It concerns women's moral autonomy and
their self-determination as opposed to the exercise of heteronomous power
by others. The woman decides for herself, not the male-dominated state,
Church or pharmaceutical industry. Women not only gain power over their
own reproductive potential but also—because of it—gain the possibility to
acquire the sources of social power owned by men. The old forms of
reproductive technology, all of which prevented reproduction, are both the
condition of and the means to accomplish freedom of choice and control
over one's own body and life.

The introduction and expansion of the new forms of reproductive
technology and the future potential of genetic manipulation have led many
feminists to reconsider this viewpoint. They recognise that the new
techniques make it possible for certain groups of women to become

mothers, such as infertile heterosexual couples, lesbian couples, single women, and couples with a probability of hereditary defects. But for them the emphasis shifts gradually towards an increasing 'medicalisation' and technological control, in the way of quantity as well as quality. I distinguish five aspects that are put forward in feminist publications.

The first aspect feminists point out is that more and more aspects of reproduction are being controlled by medical technology. While it concerned—until ten years ago—primarily the ovulation cycle, pregnancy and birth, *in vitro* fertilisation has created a breakthrough by looking at fertilisation scientifically. Also, because of this, the number of techniques regarding the foetus, sperm, and egg-cells has increased. Furthermore, partly due to IVF, fertilisation and selection techniques have started to intertwine. Reproduction and selection increasingly overlap each other.

The second aspect is part of the autonomy-versus-heteronomy issue. The reproduction experts decide which women will be considered for treatment. In the Netherlands feminists criticise the exclusion of lesbian and single women from AI and IVF treatments as a form of 'heteronomisation' and family ideology. But there is also another, less obvious, form of exclusion taking place. The number of candidates for certain techniques is gradually increasing, either through expansion of medical indications or by advertising campaigns, one of which took place in the Netherlands, which advertised information on heredity.

A third aspect of 'medicalisation' is that existential problems, such as unwanted childlessness or living with serious hereditary defects, are being redefined. They change from being philosophical to medical problems, which as a result, require medical-technical answers. Non-medical answers such as adoption, sharing the upbringing of (handicapped) children, or becoming adoptive parents, are therefore even more marginalised.

The North American sociologist Barbara Katz Rothmann and the British scholar Susan Himmelweit each indicate a fourth aspect. They suggest that it is a mere illusion to think that the freedom of choice expands with the increase of the number of technical possibilities. This optimistic view overlooks the fact that the possibility to revert to the old situation may quietly disappear because it becomes less and less socially desirable. In this way a woman's choice not to control her fertility is considered irresponsible in Western society. She defies the dominant values of control over nature, of individual development, and the ideal of a family with two children. It seems to me that the tendency to consider the choice-potential that derives from the technology as better, more progressive, and more responsible, also exists in prenatal diagnosis and selective abortion. It seems that people who decide to bring a child with hereditary defects into the world can count less and less on understanding and solidarity in a society such as the Dutch one, where good health is considered as one's highest aim.

The final aspect, related to the previous one, is the 'individualisation' of the responsibility for reproduction and for the quality of the new generation. With the expansion of individual rights and freedom comes the expansion of individual duties and responsibilities. The drawback of this development is again clearly accentuated by the application of prenatal diagnosis and selective abortion. In comparison to other forms of reproductive technology, these do not so much centre around the parent's lives, but that of the expected child. Indeed, do parents not have a moral duty to do the best for their child and avoid suffering as much as possible? If they decide against using any of these techniques—this is also a choice— and they have a handicapped child, then that is their responsibility. And possibly the mother's responsibility in particular, who is still deemed to bear the responsibility for the children's upbringing. In this way it is possible for single-parent mothers to face opposition from their child and society. The financial support for handicapped people and their nurses costs a lot of money for a society in which a certain government economy measure threatens the solidarity with vulnerable groups. The collective responsibility for the quality of living of the next generation is changed into an individual problem.

2. Freedom of choice as condition of the power of technology

The above-mentioned observations of the increasingly medical and technological control of reproduction and its consequences for women and society, raise two points. First, technology appears to be more than just a means to reach a certain goal. It is also more than a collection of techniques based on scientific research. Technology is a complex social institution with its own social structure, and with what the philosopher of science, Arnold Pacey, calls the culture or ideology of technology, an intrinsic entity interwoven with research and application, of moral values and techniques. This culture or ideology has a strong influence on the existing values in a society and, with it, on the meanings individuals attach to moral issues. Second, the feminists' call for moral autonomy and freedom of choice for women does not appear to have sufficient critical force in the face of the power of technology as a social institution. I do not mean to say that women's freedom to make choices about motherhood actually exists worldwide. It is and remains a fundamental principle of a feminist ethic. I nevertheless share the view of the Dutch ethicists H. ten Have and G. Kimsma who argue that the patient's freedom of choice and right to speak out, in other words his or her autonomy as an individual, also serves as the condition of another form of autonomy, which is the independent development of medical technology. Due to this development, on which only a small elite in science and business has any influence, the limits of what is technically possible and also ethically permissable, automatically change.

The Dutch biologist Cor van der Weele considers such a development as being a new form of eugenetics, based on the Western democratic state, in which individuals can and indeed must decide for themselves what qualities they pass on to their offspring. This is not a lawful duty but a subtle persuasion of values and meanings by the independent progressive technology. In fact, all these writers argue that reproductive technology constantly urges new values and norms—under the guise of 'autonomy' and 'self-determination'—on to society and its individual users. The individuals may choose from a number of possibilities made available by the technology, but they have no influence whatsoever on the actual choices they wish or do not wish to make.

To avoid getting entangled paradoxically with the interest of women who want to become mothers, a feminist ethic ought to address the power struggle not only in terms of autonomy and heteronomy but also in terms of what the dominant norms of society and technology regard as normal and abnormal behaviour or even the meanings of 'being'.

Also, it is no longer a question of how much women's freedom of choice and their autonomy has increased or declined. I agree with the conclusions of B. Katz Rothmann, S. Himmelweit and C. van der Weele who say that from a feminist viewpoint of reproductive technology, woman's freedom of choice should not be placed opposite, but within the context of society. This context should no longer be regarded either as an obstruction or an encouragement, but as a constituting factor which structures and orientates the choice opportunities, and also from a moral point of view. The central question is not whether choices are being created, but *how* they are created, and what factors play a role in this.

The specific contribution a feminist ethic can make to the solution of this problem seems to me to be a critical analysis and ethical evaluation of the culture of reproductive technology and of its effect on the moral dilemmas women face when they want to become a mother. From a moral theological angle this culture could of course be seen as a form of secularised belief which holds certain value-patterns as well as utopias of what success and a good life are and where perhaps even a certain image of God operates. Feminist ethicists and theologicans are concerned with the question as to what extent these values and utopias express a patriarchal ideology and what its consequences are for those women who use certain reproductive techniques. I would like to discuss this question by way of examples, *i.e.* referring to the meanings given to biological motherhood.

3. Motherhood: passive source of nutrition and rational consumer

Feminist theologians have demonstrated the relation between scientific technical control over nature and the social control over women and other 'strangers'. The woman, or rather the mother, is the primary and original image of this relation. Within the new forms of reproductive technology and genetic manipulation, this control seems to receive a new dimension. Despite the fact that the claims made by experts that *in vitro* fertilisation would eventually emulate the natural fertilisation process and that 'their' babies would be more intelligent, stronger and healthier, were wrong, they do demonstrate the desire to imitate and complete with mother nature and mother the woman. Also the 'extreme' utopias of reproducing the perfect human being and of ecto-genesis—the growth from a fertilised egg in a test-tube, to a baby—confirm that there is more to it than just the control of natural processes. In both cases nature's and women's reproductive capacity is completely absent and is replaced by high-technological processes. The human being is here a technical quality product as opposed to a piece of art.

Both these utopias shed light on yet another aspect of patriarchal ideology: the relations between humans and their environment are broken. The perfect human being who develops his character with genetically manipulated characteristics, and the foetus that no longer needs a mother for its development, reveal a certain view of mankind: that of the self-sufficient, abstract individual who lives and acts independently from his environment. The feminist psychoanalysis clearly shows that this vision of human beings is not universal, but represents the two themes characteristic of the masculine personality structure: that of separation being the condition of individuation. In a (Western) patriarchal culture a boy can only become a man if he severs the bond with his mother, and cultivates his own boundaries, regarding his environment. Both utopias very much distort the normal and normative, patriarchal view of the relation between the male and his environment in that it is characterised by a hierarchical and dualistic separation which in itself is a paradox, a non-relation. The environment—the world, the cosmos, other people, the body, and the woman—is at her best a good feeding soil; she does not contribute anything of constitutional or essential value; let alone the male being part of this environment. Here women are not so much reduced to being mothers but mothers are reduced to being a pasive environment for the foetus—and therefore the human beings—; a technical product with certain socially desirable characteristics and qualities.

This brings me to the second view of motherhood held within the culture of reproductive technology. Women who want to become a mother or are already pregnant, are increasingly treated as critical consumers, who know how to defend their rights and their expected child. They obtain and evaluate scientific information, assess the pros and cons of certain techniques and treatments before making a rational, responsible decision, which may sometimes have far-reaching and unforeseen consequences for themselves, the expected child, and their environment. Ambivalent feelings occurring before and after the decision, are (much more) considered to be 'side-effects' that women need to cope with, rather than a sign that an active and expressive attitude still does not guarantee a morally sound decision.

These conflicting images of the mother as a passive source of nutrition, for, and active controller of, the foetus have one thing in common: the relationship between the woman and her expected child is characterised by distance and separation. The focus is on the developing foetus and its quality, not on the developing relationship between mother-and-child-to-be. Both these views, therefore, are more than just future utopias. My presumption that these already have an influence on the decisions women face, as well as on the actual decision-making, is confirmed by recent research into women's experiences of prenatal diagnosis and selective abortion. In *The Tentative Pregnancy*, B. Katz Rothmann shows that women who undergo prenatal diagnosis feel forced to create a separation between themselves and the developing foetus from the start of their pregnancy, since they do not know whether or not they will successfully complete their pregnancy. While these women are pregnant, they are not expecting a child, although—and this is a complex matter—the pregnancy and the child are very much desired. The author concludes that this type of technology makes high and conflicting demands on women. Women are to conform to the masculine world of experience in which separation precedes attachment and intimacy, while the reverse takes place during pregnancy. The Dutch sociologist, Tj Tijmstra, is concerned in his research with women who are offered echoscopy because it has been established that 'something is wrong'. His report shows that some of the women feel ambivalent about this offer. They feel that they ought to use it but would have preferred not to have had the offer. Tijmstra talks of a technological imperative in this context. I would like to add that the ambivalent feelings of women do not have anything to do with a lack of responsibility, but with a burden that derives from the technological image of the mother as active and rational 'decision-maker'.

4. Conclusion

I would like to suggest the hypothesis that the aforementioned emotional and moral conflicts are not subjective and private, but are brought about by the clash between two different objective views on biological motherhood and on the relationship between the mother-to-be and the new life that is growing. Within a technological perspective, based on a patriarchal culture of hierarchical and dualistic separation between a human being and his environment, increasing value is attached to the (genetic) quality of the foetus. The mother as co-creator of new life disappears from the technological spectrum and is reduced to being a healthy source of nutrition in order to make place for the mother as active and rational consumer and co-producer.

On the other hand there is also the perspective of women themselves who, during the desired pregnancy, develop a unique as well as complex relationship of closeness and distance and of mutual dependency. It seems to me to be of great importance for a feminist ethic to achieve a deeper understanding of the various meanings and values that lie within these perspectives than I have been able to offer here. It is not a matter of making a definitive feminist judgment over whether or not a particular decision is responsible. I believe that the first step of such an analysis should be to do justice to the women and their partners who, in this sort of dilemma, struggle to reach a responsible decision. With this as starting point it is also necessary to develop a perspective on motherhood and on the relationship between mother-and-child-to-be, other than the patriarchal one. In this new perspective, 'relationship', 'creativity' and 'physicality' seem to me to be the key words for a view of motherhood which it deserves and in which the foetus is more than just a technical product or a lump of cells. I do not propose the creation of alternative utopias but the promotion of both a modest and a comprehensive, and certainly a more laborious human project: a 'small' ethic of respect in which the environment, or the other, is neither denied nor appropriated, and which is experienced and named in a way familiar to me. Such an ethic could determine the exact limits to the totalitarian demands of utopias, and celebrate the differences between people as a gift from God the Creator. With this I have formulated a fourth task and possibility for a feminist (theological) ethic of reproduction.

Translated by Vivien Hargreaves

Bibliography

Farley, M., 'Feminist Theology and Bioethics,' in B. Hilkert Andelson, C. Gudorf and M. Pellauer (eds.), *Women's Consciousness, Women's Conscience: A Reader in Feminist Ethics* (San Francisco 1985, pp. 285–305.

Have, H. ten and Kimsma G., *Geneeskunde tussen droom an drama*; Voortplanting, ethiek en vooruitgang (Kampen 1987).

Heyward, C., 'The Limits of Liberalism; Feminism in moral crisis', in C. Heyward, *Our Passion for Justice: Images of Power, Sexuality and Liberation* (New York 1984), pp. 153–174.

Himmelweit S., 'More than "A Woman's Right to Choose"?',*Feminist Review* 29 (Spring 1988), pp. 38–56.

Katz Rothmann, B., 'Choice in Reproductive Technology', in R. Arditti, R. Duelli Kleir and S. Minden (eds.), *Test-Tube Women: What Future for Motherhood?* (London 1984), pp. 23–35; *Idem., The Tentative Pregnancy: Prenatal Diagnosis and the Future of Motherhood* (London 1986).

Pacey, A., *The Culture of Technology* (Cambridge 1983).

Praetorius, I., 'Theologische Ethik-feministische Theologie-Frauenpolitik', in M. Brockskotheen (ed.), *Frauen gegen Gentechnik und Reproduktionstechnik* (Köln 1986), pp. 95–97.

Tijmstra, Tj., 'De beleving van echoscopisch enderziek', *Medisch Contact* 42 (1987), pp. 464–466.

Weele, C. van der, 'Eugenetica in een nieuw jasje?', *Tijdschrift voor gezondheid on politiek* (December 1985), pp. 25–27.

Wildung Harrison B., with S. Cleyes, 'Theology and Morality of Procreative Choice', in C. Robb (ed.), *Making the Connections: Essays in Feminist Social Ethics* (Boston 1985), pp. 115–134.

Mary Condren

To Bear Children for the Fatherland: Mothers and Militarism

THE WORDS of one of the closing addresses to women at the Second Vatican Council have never ceased to give me pause for thought. 'Women of the entire universe, you to whom life is entrusted, it is for you to save the peace of the world.' On the face of it, these were noble sentiments, a recognition of the place of women in Catholic theology. But the context in which they were spoken belies, and radically undermines, the sentiments expressed. For women had hardly been allowed to speak at this event, even on the subject of saving the world.

The statement epitomises the double jeopardy into which women have been placed in Western culture. On the one hand, women are expected to become the repositories and safeguarders of morality, a position uniquely accorded to them by their experience of mothering. Yet when women try to extend their moral consciousness into the wider political or religious world where it may have serious effect, their 'femininity', the basis upon which their superior moral stance appears to rest, is all but said to disappear.

The dilemma was nowhere better expressed than in recent years in Ireland with the 'Peace Women'. When thousands of women marched through the streets of Ireland crying 'peace' their leaders were awarded the Nobel Peace Prize. When the same women, realising there could be no peace without justice, set out to develop a concrete programme of action to address social inequity, their support dwindled to a trickle. They had become 'political'; they had lost their 'peace' platform, and for all intents and purposes, they may as well have lost their honour.

In recent years, the enormity of the nuclear threat has generated many new studies of warfare and of the complex role played by gender politics. Is there a relationship, natural or otherwise, between women and peace? Is this relationship one that can be used to bring about peace, or is it simply a foil to disguise and even legitimate the death-dealing of modern statecraft? Why, for instance, do nations devote so much of their financial and cultural resources to the preservation of the war machinery and so little to institutes devoted to the study of peacemaking? If wars are indeed waged for the 'defence of women and children', why is so little public money spent on rape crisis centres who deal on a daily basis with the on-going war against women and children waged by patriarchal sexual attitudes and practices? There are some very curious contradictions around the issues of women, peace, and defence, that need much further exploration.

While in the thought of the Vatican and certain strands of the feminist movement women might be 'natural' pacifists, historically, the evidence on the role of women in warfare is ambivalent. While it would be true to say that women have seldom, if ever, initiated war, in the animal kingdom there is no fiercer animal than a mother protecting her young. In the major European wars women have worked in the ancillary services in roles ranging from nursing to concentration camp supervisors. In contemporary warfare, especially in those wars of 'liberation', women play an active part as combatants, and indeed today the question is often raised as to whether women's liberation should automatically make them liable for conscription and combat duty.

Quite aside from their actual roles in warfare, women have played a variety of symbolic roles. Women have acted as 'pretexts for war', 'recompense for the allies', 'valuables' that need to be defended, guarantors of 'the warrior's rest and recreation', nurses, and cheerleaders, 'miracle mothers', 'wistful wives', 'treacherous tramps', and 'co-operative citizens'. Women's role on the battlefield has been so all-pervasive that the contemporary theorist Nancy Huston has commented that 'if women were not "present in their absence" on the battlefield, *nothing would happen there worth writing about*'.[1]

Mothers of soldiers traditionally have taken pride in seeing their sons march off to war as though their willingness to fight proved their manhood. Some mothers support their son's military involvement on the grounds that the military will 'take care' of their sons, especially those the women found hard to discipline.[2]

Even where they are not actively involved in war efforts women play a role as the 'witnesses' to men's heroism. Women have acted as 'mirrors' reflecting back to men double their original size.[3] As Tacitus wrote,

Close by them, too, are those who are dearest to them, so that they hear the shrieks of women, the cries of infants. They [women] are to every man the most sacred witnesses of his bravery—they are the most generous applauders. The soldier brings his wounds to his mother and his wife . . .[4]

Perhaps women's greatest act of witness to men's warrior deeds lies in her act of mourning. From earliest times the 'mourning' of women has played a crucial role in warfare. When the ancient religious rites of Greece were abolished in favour of those of the state, the only rites remaining to women were the women's wail, left to 'accompany the fall of the victim in the great blood sacrifice'.[5] When one of the hunger strikers in Ireland died several years ago a fellow republican prisoner wrote a tribute to his wife:

> . . . she despaired not. She bore the pain and took comfort from the fact that Joe was faithful and he fought. In sharing the grief of Goretti McDonnell we share in the grief of every bereaved Irish mother or wife. From time immemorial, from their courage we draw new strength.[6]

And even though women rarely *invent* war tales, throughout the ages and through various ancestral rites, they have acted successfully as transmitters of the heroic deeds of men.[7]

Participation in warfare has conveyed very dubious 'benefits' to women. In medieval times, women's right to hold property was made conditional upon her willingness to 'defend' herself.[8] Similarly, although many early suffragists were anti-war, they also were quick to recognise the benefits women's participation in warfare had brought to them, including the enfranchisement they had sought for so long.[9]

War also provides an escape valve when the inherent violence of patriarchal social relations threatens to overspill allowing this violence to escape temporarily and 'emigrate' without destroying the sexual relations of those societies in which it is situated. For men it offers an escape from 'civilisation', in which all the pent-up hostility against the 'Other' in their lives can be directed at alternative enemies abroad. Women can temporarily lose their quality of 'Otherness' in warfare, enter the public world and reject the stifling domesticity to which their role as men's 'Other' has confined them.[10]

Given the evidence, we must conclude that women are not 'naturally' pacifists. Nevertheless, their involvement in warfare, at whatever level, represents a profound tragedy. For warfare, more than any other institution, plays a powerful role in the generation of symbolic capital for patriarchal culture in which their self-interest as women is constantly and radically undermined.

Patriarchal societies thrive on the establishment of dualisms; between men and women, the sacred and profane, and between the public and the private. These dualisms do not come naturally, but must be maintained through periodic exhortations, philosophical discourse, and ritual. Warfare provides the occasion for all three.

Throughout warfare and the training of soldiers, the hatred of women and of what they represent plays a major role in enabling soldiers to forge their identities. Soldiers are often insulted by their commanding officers with such epithets as 'vagina-face', 'used sanitary napkin', 'abortion', or 'miscarriage'. Indeed one of the central tactics of warrior training is the questioning of a soldier's manhood, which he will then go to any lengths, usually violent, to defend. For men do not just become 'men', they become 'Not-Women'.[11]

The world of the soldier is essentially a 'barracks community', where as far as possible any traces of women's influence are eliminated.[12] Ideally the barracks community is homosexual. Plato held that homosexual lovers would be invincible, and he regretted that it was not possible to turn cowardly soldiers into women.[13] Even the peace-loving Wilfrid Owen spoke of women with a certain contempt. As he wrote in one of his letters to his mother: 'All women, without exception, *annoy* me.'[14]

In the most explicit initiation rites of tribal warriors, some young men actually step on their mother's bellies in a gesture signifying their successful initiation or individuation. Some soldiers talk of their 'freedom' from the 'stuffiness' of drawingrooms, or the restraints of civilisation represented by women, while in one of his marching songs, A. E. Housman sings happily: 'Woman bore me/ I will rise.'

It has even been argued that the patriarchal discourses generated during the First World War were a direct response to the early suffragist movement, the first serious threat that patriarchal social relations had experiences, and that had threatened the 'manhood' of the society, a threat that had already found expression in an increased incidence of violence against, and male resentment of women.[15] In the discourses of the major world wars 'manhood' and 'nationality' are almost synonymous. As Patrick Pearse wrote at that time, echoing sentiments to be found throughout Europe: 'bloodshed is a cleansing and sanctifying thing, and the nation which regards it as the final horror has lost its *manhood*' (emphasis added).[16]

During warfare the male can successfully project his fear of women, or fear of the insecurity of his manhood, onto a superior male represented by the government. Men's social identity is forged in the sacred world of battle, a world that becomes sacred because it is freed from the polluting influences of women. Men who would otherwise be doomed to social inferiority or ignominy, and those who identify with them, can through their warrior efforts be elevated to hero status transcending, even for the moment, class and economic barriers, and becoming, through their willingness to sacrifice, automatically superior to the other half of the human race.[17] Ideally, however, for manhood to be equated with sacrality, wars will be fought on behalf of God, or certainly with God 'on their side'.

In the legitimating efforts of states war veterans, and the cult of the war-dead, now play a powerful symbolic role. Monuments to the 'Unknown Soldier' who 'gave his all' now, throughout Europe, replace those once erected to the dead Christ 'who died for all'. The sacrifices of war often now replace sacrifices on the altar.

The gendered split between the sacred and the profane is paralleled by the split between public and private life. The ancient Greeks and their contemporary followers such as Kant and Hegel, decided that women were a decided impediment to the life of the *polis*. Women, they argued, were incapable of transcending their particularistic interests, rooted in the care of their families, to sacrifice themselves for the 'Common Good'. Only men were considered capable of achieving the degree of ethical abstraction necessary to see the whole, and the proof of their ethical consciousness was their willingness to lay down their lives. Indeed according to Immanuel Kant, 'perpetual peace' would be the greatest threat to ethical consciousness, while George Fredrich Hegel's master/slave paradigm of the state and the need for constant 'transcendence', could lead to nothing less than perpetual warfare.

In the ideal patriarchal state women will inhabit only the domestic world. Warfare, according to political philosophers, is fundamentally incompatible with self-love or with the protection of one's own self-interests. As Mary O'Brien argues, according to political philosophers, women could not become part of the state because of their 'unheroic and irrational objection to the slaughter of their own children'.[18] But in the last analysis, patriarchal ethics depend upon perpetual warfare for their continued existence.[19]

Given the multitude of roles that women play in war, the seeming benefits to be derived therefrom, and yet the overwhelming evidence of the role of warfare in generating symbolic capital for the continuing oppression of women, how can we begin to talk about the relationship between women and peace, or must women forever bear children for the fatherland? Faced with the overwhelming threat of nuclear destruction we have little choice but to maintain that there is such a relationship, however tenuous. But given the historical manipulation of this relationship, we also have to maintain that, far from being 'natural', the relationship is one that must be worked at, laboured over, and extracted like a screaming newborn from the morass of contemporary sexual politics.

The myth of the 'natural' peacefulness of women has carried with it several implications. First, logically, if women are 'naturally' pacifist then nothing in their social conditions, or conditioning, needs to be changed. Not surprisingly, this situation suits those who wish to maintain the patriarchal *status quo*. Second, the ideology of women's 'natural' pacifism has historically served to maintain the myth of women's powerlessness. Third, women's moral purity has been gained, and is now maintained, at the cost of its political effectiveness. Let us examine each of these in turn.

Quite apart from the symbolic and actual roles women play in warfare, feminist theorists are now seriously proposing that maternal practice 'is as conducive to battle as to peace'.[20] In particular, the cult of motherhood with its attendant ideology of self-denial and sexual repression, far from encouraging social equilibrium, may be doing precisely the opposite. Women's lack of a clearly defined 'self-interest' leaves them in a moral vacuum. On the one hand, their selflessness confines them to the home, the world of domestic decision making, and on the other, on the one occasion where they are allowed to enter the political world in times of war, their selflessness is then expended on the profoundly selfish adventures of nationalists and patriots. Not taking responsibility for, or having any clear articulation of, their erotic or other needs, these can then be exploited in the service of the war machine. Like some of the early suffragists they confuse the 'national interest' with their own, preventing the international bonding and co-operation of women on terms that would genuinely support their self-interests as generators and sustainers of the human race and defenders of human life.

The cult of motherhood carries with it the myth of women's powerlessness. In turn, this prevents women from studying the kinds of power we do have, and reduces us to a condition of moral imbecility in the use of that power. The myth of women's powerlessness and selflessness, in particular, prevents women from coming to terms with the profoundly political nature of child rearing practices.

Feminist theory is increasingly finding correlations between rigidly defined sex roles and institutional violence.[21] Hierarchical societies depend crucially on their boundary definitions and a premium is, therefore, laid upon male aggression enabling, as it does, these boundaries to be maintained. In turn, the more boundaries need to be maintained, the more this will be reflected in child rearing practices.

Recent studies of the childrearing involved in such persons as Adolf Hitler, and contemporary terrorists, indicate clearly that their early childhood experiences of violence predisposes such future adults to violence and revenge, either on their own children, or on society at large. In some cases, such as that of Hitler, the need for revenge is insatiable and the need to redress childhood traumas wreaks future havoc on the social world.[22]

While Hitler may be an extreme example, other evidence now indicates that even the more 'normal' childrearing practices can have devastating impact on the social world. In particular, women who buy into the myth of their own powerlessness, who have no sense of selfworth, become incapable of conferring an enabling form of recognition upon their children allowing them successfully to individuate. Their female children will usually react to this by emulating their mothers's behaviour, thereby passing it on to the next generation. Their lack of self esteem makes them particularly prone to becoming 'co-dependants' of substance abusers, and vulnerable to the physical and psychological abusiveness of the submission/domination syndrome.[23]

Women's loss of self also produces misogynistic sons who, in the process of their own separation from their mothers, and faced with the 'non-being' of their mother's femaleness, desperately define themselves as 'Not-Women', and search furiously for a compensatory, revengeful, and exaggerated male identity that often finds violent expression.[24]

The myth of women's moral purity has been gained, and is now maintained, at the cost of its political effectiveness. Keeping women out of the life of the city, seemingly powerless, and pathologically 'unselfish', has been the most effective way of ensuring their loss of control over that which has traditionally been most precious to them: the lives of their own children. Their moral purity is vitiated at its source.

In return for the unquestioning acceptance of the myth of women's moral purity, and the myth of women's powerlessness, women receive 'protection'. It is precisely the nature of this protection that women need to suspect and criticise, given that the discourse of 'protection' is operative throughout and legitimates the war machine, and its daily equivalent: rape.[25]

There is then, no essential relationship between women and peace, and those who argue there is, are usually engaging in manipulative and mystifying rhetoric designed to maintain the sexual *status quo*. In addition, they are often guilty of indulging in false compensation practices such as the idealisation of 'true womanhood', or the claim that the real object of their warrior enterprises is protection of the 'motherland'.

Any discussion of women's role in peacemaking, therefore, must arise, not from an idealist or theological category as to woman's 'true nature', but must come from the praxis of women's lives. Several theorists have recently proposed one way forward as the systematisation of 'maternal thinking', in order to extrapolate from women's roles in the private world, based on 'preservative and attentive love', to the public world.[26]

Feminist theorists stress the dangers inherent in this enterprise, the dangers of inauthenticity, and in particular, the danger of establishing a new idealism. 'Maternal thinking' is a 'moral activity rather than a virtue achieved'.[27] It is at once a spiritual practice, akin to non-violence training, and an attempt to develop on a par with the Marxist analyses of production, an epistemology of the politics of reproduction and its effect on the public and private world.

As the feminist movement has claimed from the beginning, 'the personal is political', and perhaps now for the first time in human history these traditional dualisms can be reconciled with the aid of a theology that is respectful of the real roles women and men play in the world and of the political and theological consequences arising therefrom.

Notes

1. Nancy Huston, 'Tales of War and Tears of Women', *Women's Studies International Forum* 5 (1982), 275.
2. Linda Rennie Forcey, 'Making of Men in the Military: Perspectives From Mothers', *Women's Studies International Forum* 6:6 (1984), 478, 484.
3. Judith Hicks Stiehm, 'The Protected, the Protector, the Defender', *Women's Studies International Forum* 5:3/4 (1982), 370.
4. Cited in Mary Beard, *Women as Force in History* (1947; New York 1972), p. 289.
5. Jean Pierre-Vernant and Pierre Vidal-Naquet, *Tragedy and Myth in Ancient Greece* (Sussex 1981), p. 16.
6. Cited in Eileen Fairweather *et al.*, *Only Our Rivers Run Free: Northern Ireland: The Women's War* (London 1984), pp. 101–102.
7. Huston, 'Tales of War', 275.
8. Mary Condren, *The Serpent and the Goddess: Women, Religion and Power in Celtic Ireland* (San Francisco 1989), p. 64.
9. Betty Rozak and Theodore Rozak, eds., *Masculine/Feminine: Readings in Sexual Mythology and the Liberation of Women* (New York 1969), p. 98.
10. Jean Bethke Elshtain, 'Woman, Mirror and Other: Toward a Theory of Women, War and Feminism', *Humanities in Society* 5:1/2 (1982), 39.
11. See Nancy Jay, 'Gender and Dichotomy', *Feminist Studies* 7:1 (1981), 38–56.
12. See Nancy Hartsock, 'The Barracks Community in Western Political Thought: Prologomena to a Feminist Critique of War and Politics', *Women's Studies International Forum* 5 (1982), 283–286.
13. Sara Ruddick, 'Preservative Love and Military Destruction: Some Reflections

on Mothering and Peace', in *Mothering: Essays in Feminist Theory*, ed. Joyce Trebilcot, (Totowa, NJ 1984), p. 253; Plato, *The Laws* (Harmondsworth 1970 edn.), s. 944.

14. Wilfrid Owen, *Collected Letters*, ed. Harold Owen and John Bell (London 1967), p. 274. Cited in Caryn McTighe Musil, 'Wilfrid Owen and Abram', *Women's Studies* 13 (1986), 60.
15. Roszak and Roszak, *op. cit.*, p. 95.
16. Patrick Pearse, *Collected Works: Political Writings and Speeches* (Dublin 1924), p. 99.
17. See Nancy Jay, 'Sacrifice as Remedy for Having Been Born of Woman', in *Immaculate and Powerful: The Female in Sacred Image and Social Reality*, eds. Clarissa Atkinson *et al.* (Boston 1985), pp. 283–309.
18. Mary O'Brien, *The Politics of Reproduction* (London 1981), p. 148.
19. Jo-Ann Pilardi Fuchs, 'On the War Path and Beyond: Hegel, Freud and Feminist Theory', *Women's Studies International Forum* 6:6 (1983), 566. See also, Edith Wyschogrod, *Spirit in Ashes: Hegel, Heidegger and Man-Made Death* (New Haven 1985).
20. Ruddick, 'Preservative Love', p. 255.
21. Riane Eisler, 'Violence and Male Dominance: The Ticking Time Bomb', *Humanities in Society* 7:1/2 (1984), 5–6.
22. See Alice Miller, *For Your Own Good: Hidden Cruelty in Child-Rearing and the Roots of Violence*, trans. Hildegarde and Hunter Hannum, (New York 1984). *Am Anfang war Erziehung* (Frankfurt am Main 1980).
23. See Jessica Benjamin, *The Bonds of Love: Psychoanalysis, Feminism and the Problem of Domination* (New York 1988).
24. Nancy Hartsock, *Money, Sex and Power: Toward a Feminist Historical Materialism* (Boston 1985), pp. 169, 177. See also, Nancy Chodorow, *The Reproduction of Mothering: Psychoanalysis and the Sociology of Gender* (Berkeley 1978); Dorothy Dinnerstein, *The Mermaid and the Minotaur: Sexual Arrangements and Human Malaise* (New York 1977).
25. Jean Bethke Elshtain, 'On Beautiful Souls, Just Warriors and Feminist Consciousness', *Women's Studies International Forum* 3/4 (1982), 342.
26. Sara Ruddick, 'Maternal Thinking', in *Mothering: Essays in Feminist Theory* ed. Joyce Trebilcot, p. 221.
27. Ruddick, 'Preservative Love', p. 239.

Catharina Halkes

The Rape of Mother Earth: Ecology and Patriarchy

THIS ESSAY consists of three parts: the shift from an organic vision of the earth, nature and the universe to a mechanistic way of looking at things in which nature is regulated by external factors and matter is merely something dead and lifeless; theological reflections on the effect of Gen. 1:26–28 and some impulses for a renewed theology of creation; and some notes on patriarchy, feminism and ecology.

1. From organic vision to mechanistic interpretation

Of old people experienced their world, nature, the earth and the entire universe as holy, as an interconnected reality that was both *fascinosum et tremendum*. There was a mysterious order to be experienced in the change of day and night, of ebb and flood, of sun and moon, of the seasons. In all ancient cultures and religions this mystery of ordered organisation and fruitfulness is symbolised in the image of the Great Mother. The well-known student of comparative religion Gerardus van der Leeuw wrote of the figure of the mother: 'There is nothing more sacred on earth than the worship of the mother, which leads us back to the deepest secret in our soul, the relation of mother and child. She is the most mysterious figure of God.'[1] God the Father, the masculine God, is a newcomer; the son as hero and redeemer is earlier. This Great Mother exists under many figures and many names: she is the world mother, the queen of heaven, and mother earth. As late as the palaeolithic period this latter image involved the entire universe and did not then include any sexual polarisation: human beings thought of themselves then as being in her lap, which provided them with both security and food. But later this image could be used in a more restricted sense, of mother earth as opposed to heaven as masculine and paternal, with the two sexes being symbolised: the seed of heaven was poured into the womb of the earth in the form of dew or rain and fertility was thus guaranteed.[2]

To put it another way, the fundamental metaphor that linked the individual human being, society and the universe was that of an organism which expressed the mutual dependence that was present in every sphere. The earth was experienced as a living organism, sensitive with regard to all human activity. In all its organic vitality it was compared with the human body and in particular with the female body, whose womb fed all life and provided what was needed.

Because human beings gradually no longer felt themselves to be enfolded by the Great Mother but regarded themselves as living *on* the earth, a certain distancing from the earth arose which led to debate about the admissibility of intervention in her body. Not only in classical antiquity but up till the end of the Middle Ages voices of dissuasion and warning were to be heard, for example with regard to mining, which uses technology to capture more artificially from mother earth the precious treasures which she keeps hidden in her lap and allows to grow organically. This intervention is then seen as procuring an abortion.[3]

The Indian understanding of life, which has always been opposed to interventions that are literally incisions in the body of mother earth, thus existed in our own culture too. Miners have long brought offerings and sought forgiveness in their prayers for penetrating the womb of the earth.

Debate in this field from classical antiquity onwards centred round three subjects: the lawfulness of violating the earth and bringing to light what it had been holding and preserving hidden away; the 'ecological' consequences of, for example, felling trees, deforestation and the pollution of rivers; and finally opposition to greed and male lust.

We must however acknowledge that over against the positive image of nature as a kind and nourishing mother there was also a negative image: nature as savage, wild, unpredictable and ungovernable, capable of causing violence and chaos. This image too was experienced as 'feminine' and slowly began to obtain more influence. Up to the sixteenth century the positive image of mother earth prevailed: it called for respect and restraint with regard to human intervention. But then the expansive delight in enterprise, in commerce and technology asserted itself and the tension between the experience of nature as worthy of respect and nature as untrustworthy became too great. The image of mother earth had to give way to that of nature as 'wild' and asking to be tamed. Norms and values thus shifted.

Through the victory of a more mechanistic way of looking at the world as a whole the mastering of nature came more and more into focus. The warnings mentioned above (including those of the Roman Pliny) against greed were thus explained, but in order to understand those directed against lust it is necessary to establish that the female body still always provided the image of nature. John Donne (1573–1631) wrote in his elegy 'To his mistris going to bed':

> Licence my roaving hands, and let them go,
> Before, behind, between, above, below.
> O my America! my new-found-land . . .[4]

Lust and physical love for the female body are associated with the shafts and pits in which the miner sought his gold. And this America is then the symbol and reality of the newly discovered country with its 'wild' tracts of land and people, its 'virgin' forests: it can be conquered, raped and exploited and the killing of its inhabitants provides the blood to fertilise its soil.

Finally there is the image of nature as means of escape from work that continually occupies people more and more. That is represented by a nymph in idyllic pastoral surroundings, already unveiled but wholly passive, ready to comfort tired men.

In and through the revolutions that characterise the seventeenth century we also see the transition from an organic metaphor of the mother who feeds and protects to the metaphor of a machine, a mechanism, an external factor, applied by man to conquer her either in her passivity or in her 'wildness' and to rob her of her riches.[5]

This marks the start of the 'masculine birth of time', the title of an early work by one of the founding fathers of the new empirical physical sciences, Francis Bacon, Lord Verulam (1561–1626). In his expressive language the association of nature with the passive female body becomes more than clear. In *De dignitate et augmentis scientiarum* Bacon writes:

> Neither am I of opinion in this history of marvels that superstitious narratives of sorceries, witchcrafts, charms, dreams, divinations, and the like, where there is an assurance and clear evidence of the fact, should be altogether excluded . . . Howsoever the use and practice of such arts is to be condemned, yet from the speculation and consideration of them . . . a useful light may be gained, not only for a true judgment of the

offences of persons charged with such practices, but likewise for the further disclosing of the secrets of nature. Neither ought a man to make scruple of entering and penetrating into these holes and corners, when the inquisition of truth is his whole object.[6]

One of Bacon's posts was that of attorney general at the time when King James VI and I was intensifying the laws against witches. He knew very well what was meant by inquisition. Carolyn Merchant summarises his views as follows, citing his *Novum Organon* and *The Great Instauration*:

The new method of interrogation was not through abstract notions, but through the instruction of the understanding 'that it may in very truth dissect nature'. The instruments of the mind supply suggestions, those of the hand give motion and aid the work. 'By art and the hand of man', nature can then be 'forced out of her natural state and squeezed and moulded'. In this way, 'human knowledge and human power meet as one'.[7]

Even in his earliest work we come across the now well-known words: 'I am come in very truth leading to you nature with all her children to bind her to your service and make her your slave.'[8]

In complete agreement with the social transformations aimed at restoring women to being a psychic and reproductive resource once again, Bacon developed the power of language as a political instrument in order to reduce 'feminine nature' to a resource for economic production. He called the union of science and nature 'a chaste and lawful marriage' in which the power of 'the man' and the passivity of 'the woman' found expression.

After the development of the empirical natural sciences the rationalism of the new thought must also be mentioned. Descartes was the great father of this. The human intellect alone now became the *res cogitans* and all the rest—nature, the universe, the corporeal and material world—became merely *res extensae*, extension, the object of the knowing intellect. Nature thus became mind-less, spirit-less, and human beings through their rational knowledge could become its *maîtres et possesseurs*. The dualism between man and nature that thus arose is obvious: nature was seen merely as extension and the mind that perceived it was without extension.

Of course with this brief description of the thought of Bacon and Descartes I am not doing justice to the importance of their work. All I am concerned with here is the down-grading of nature and, in the case of Bacon, the association of nature with domination of the female element. Western philosophy and natural science from now on began developing in a direction which on the one hand has led to impressive results and on the other has caused the alienation of man from nature and ultimately has been at the expense of mother earth and the entire environment.

2. Towards a renewed theology of creation

It is striking that not only philosophers followed this path but that theologians, too, wholeheartedly agreed with this development. We see this become apparent particularly in the views of the theology of secularisation. Here are just a few examples: 'All technology expresses dominion over things and thus over nature. The ancient mythical saying: "Subdue the earth" has been fulfilled by technology' (Tillich, 1927). A. van Leeuwen has as the main theme of his *Christianity in World History* the idea that 'the cosmic tree that represents the living universe', image of ontocracy, must give way before technocracy, the fruit of Judaism and Christianity. Levinas too advocates the destruction of all 'sacred groves'.[9] Both anxiety about becoming fascinated by nature (the tree of life) and the work-ethic play their part here in the thinking of predominantly Protestant theologians.

Only through the ecological crisis has the idea been awakened that the Christian theology of creation has been insufficiently developed and has insufficient powers of expression. This deficiency is expressed in the implicit criticism of the ancient nature-religions contained in the biblical accounts of creation whereby creation becomes understood merely as 'separating' and the figure of the mother has disappeared. As a result the covenant, particularly in Protestant theology, has gained priority over creation. Karl Barth (and many after him) regards creation as the 'external ground' of the covenant and the covenant as the 'internal ground' of creation. What is internal is the essence, what is external the periphery. In this way creation becomes merely the start of the history of the covenant and can only be understood on the basis of the covenant, and thus on the basis of history.[10] (Barth was later to adopt a somewhat modified position.)

Not only was human nature of small worth in the Protestant confession of faith but there was also a strong ambivalence with regard to nature as a whole. Catholic theology remained more positive in this respect and recognised God's traces in creation. In Vatican II's pastoral constitution *Gaudium et spes* there is strong emphasis on human responsibility for the whole of creation. It is striking that of recent years Protestant theologians are making up this lost ground, as is shown by important works by among others Moltmann, Liedke, and Altner.[11]

In the third place the interpretation of 'subduing the earth' and 'dominion' in Gen. 1:28 has been an obstacle to reaching a better understanding of our responsibility with regard to the whole of creation. Being made in the image of God was thought to consist of ruling like God over the earth and this ruling was then seen in the patriarchal sense as domination. Bacon and Descartes were believers who thought that when human beings had fuller knowledge they were also in a position to rule in this way: knowledge is power.

A new theological approach is marked by important elements which can make the theology of creation stronger and more complete. Here I can only mention them without developing them:

(1) Creation is not merely 'separating' but is also the ordering of what exists and the giving of creative impulses. This is developed above all in process theology.

(2) Creation is a theological category of its own, intended for *all* men and women and for the whole world. It should not be regarded as a category derived from the covenant.

(3) In usual talk of the six days of creation the sabbath is totally forgotten, the day pre-eminently of release from work. 'And God rested from the work of his hands and saw that it was good.' This points to a more contemplative attitude in which God, humankind and the world are linked to each other.[12]

(4) Alongside God's action of redemption and liberation which has had all the emphasis, we must also bring God's action of blessing back into our attention. The psalms are full of it. The emphasis thus falls also on what may be called the durative aspect of God's action that keeps everything in being and protects it. In addition the cyclical aspect of creation, of birth, growth and decay, regains its proper value.[13]

(5) In place of the completely transcendent monotheistic God, almost separated from 'his' creation, more attention is now being paid again to the aspect of relationship in the internal life of the Godhead, the *perichoresis* of the three divine persons, the communication and solidarity both internally and externally and thus also with regard to creation and the world. The Godhead becomes more cosmic and its immanence in our world is expressed and recognised. Moltmann in particular is compelling on this panentheism.

(6) In the language of image and metaphor with which a new metaphorical theology is concerned, the metaphor has been developed of the world as the body of God (compare the Church as the body of Christ), an image which intensifies our involvement in and responsibility for this world that God has created and increases the worth of our corporeality.[14] It is perhaps

significant that the writers referred to here are women who, as is also shown by many publications from the field of feminist theology, are concerned to resist polarisation, dualism and separation in order to ask for attention to be paid to connectedness and inter-relationship, between God and the world, God and human beings, and human beings and creation.[15]

(7) Finally a transition can be detected from an anthropocentric (or rather in fact an androcentric) theology of creation to an ecological one which has as its starting point the interdependence of everything that lives and moves throughout the whole of creation.

3. Patriarchy, feminism and ecology

It is particularly the last two points that bring us to the third section of this essay. My position is that as long as patriarchy endures an ecology that leads to real change is impossible.

In this context I define patriarchy in a broad sense and understand by it: (a) the organisation of society as a pyramid, with those in power and authority at the top and underneath a structure depending on a chain of command and obedience; (b) the mentality that is the consequence of this thinking of power as domination and regarding men (mind) as superior to women (body); (c) striving for progress and mastery, if necessary at the expense of others—'inferiors', women, other races and regions, nature itself.[16]

What is involved in patriarchy is not in the first instance individual men but a social system that is dominated by men (the fathers). It concerns the social construction of reality (the building up of society)—the significance, value and judgments that are applied to what is happening in society (the culture or civilisation)—and finally it concerns a constructed symbolic universe, a 'sacred canopy' which expresses the way in which people think about religious and cosmic reality and how they project their values and norms on to this background. For this reason the feminist protest against the image of God as Father was necessary because the dominant culture had developed this image according to its own ideal and had made it subservient to that.

Before theology reacted to the ecological crisis two new movements had come into being and taken the lead: the ecological movement and the new women's movement, feminism. Both shared an egalitarian perspective: the ecological movement developed an ecological ethic which depended on the mutual interrelationship between humankind and its environment; the feminist movement had as its primary aim to liberate women from the alienation that had been imposed on them so that they could reach an authentic understanding of themselves and to make them aware of their own roots and personal experiences. Because of this it was able to catch sight of the fate of all other marginalised groups, declare its solidarity with them and finally in this way realise their inter-relationship with the whole of creation.

Environmental problems are ultimately societal problems and form a sub-section of a particular social system. Hence they can only be grasped in the light of the historical development of that society. It is not technology but society itself that is the problem, its culture, the values and norms that it has established, and the economy that it operates. It is the dominant culture or civilisation itself that has allowed science and technology, originally means of amassing knowledge for the benefit of all, to become independent and almost impossible to pin down or come to grips with.

For women it is necessary to dig down to a deeper layer in these matters because it is a matter of social problems. Precisely because we have been excluded from culture we have acquired experiences which are now relevant: perseverance, patience, solidarity with daily and other cyclical rhythms, and above all facing up realistically and soberly to the way things are going. All this does not form part of our 'feminine nature' but is the result of the way patriarchy assigned roles to us and made us invisible for so long.

Now that we realise this properly we can shake off the possible internalisation that has been the consequence of this, rise up and take our place as people who contribute to the culture of our society and who moreover want to go on living in connectedness and association with nature.

The ecological movement and the women's movement are therefore most profoundly subversive, offering a critique of the dominant culture and wanting to bring about its transformation. What in fact is involved here is a protest against unbridled progress that pays no attention to the consequences; a protest against the lethal rivalry in which people begrudge each other life; a protest against the aggressive style of action in the world economy without regard to the number of countries in the Third World that are the victims of this; a protest against the exploitation of the earth, of the environment, without listening to the warnings these are giving; a protest against the dominant linear way of thinking that pays no attention to the rhythm of the cyclic life of nature and humankind; and finally it involves a protest against the impossibility of getting to grips with the political and economic powers thanks to their abstract language that is designed for concealment, thanks to their complex financial arrangements and the enormous scale these are on, and thanks to their life-sapping bureaucracy.

Of course it makes sense for these movements—and I include the peace movement here too—to exercise pressure 'from below' and thus to gain power through influencing people, through making people aware and through protest. But we shall need to look further and develop strategies for a 'grassroots economy', for an economy with a human face, and for a spirituality of compassion that reaches out to all who are marginalised, including the environment. It is a question now of 'eco' and no longer of 'ego'.[17]

Only one answer is possible, not only to the question of how we can survive but above all to the fundamental question of how we can live with each other in another way and reach a convivial society. The answer is: when patriarchy disappears; when it gives up its practices of power and thus the oppression of innumerable people; when it abandons war as an instrument of conquest and as a means of solving differences; and when it gives up its mental pictures, its thinking in stereotypes, particularly where women are concerned.

Women are still always associated with 'nature', with their body, with their womb; and men with culture, power, and conquest. Men have been socialised so profoundly that they are afraid of their body, of nature, of decay and of death. They project all this on the female body. While men have for ages been the masters of our reproductive capacity, the danger is now not imaginary that in an excessive technological application of science they may once again make themselves the masters of the woman's womb, see the procreation of children as a medical matter (hence 'culture') and set the tone once again.

Whenever women today take part in science and technology they can only contribute to the fall of patriarchy if they do not adapt or compromise but remain loyal to their own presuppositions.

On the basis of this kind of attitude fruitful co-operation is conceivable between all who form part of the ecological and women's movements: an arena for men and women to listen to each other and by working through the ecological problems to touch the roots of our true humanity: to remain true to nature, to listen to it and thus to create an ecological culture in which there is room for everyone and everything.

Ultimately patriarchy is not something predestined but a historical phenomenon. It arose at some time; it can also disappear again. And it is now the time for that . . .

Translated by Robert Nowell

Notes

1. G. van der Leeuw, *Phänomenologie der Religion* (Tübingen [3]1970), pp. 86 ff.
2. *Cf.* Jürgen Moltmann, *Gott in der Schöpfung* (Munich [2]1985), pp. 300ff.

3. Carolyn Merchant, *The Death of Nature* (San Francisco 1980), p. 7.
4. Quoted in Merchant, *op. cit.*, pp. 40–41.
5. Merchant, chapter 1, *passim.*
6. Quoted in Merchant, *op. cit.*, p. 168.
7. Merchant, *op. cit.*, p. 171.
8. Francis Bacon, *The Masculine Birth of Time*, ed. and tr. Benjamin Farrington (Liverpool 1964), p. 62, quoted by Merchant, *op. cit*, p. 170.
9. *Cf.* Hans Achterhuis, 'De boom des levens: mythe of realiteit?', in Hans Achterhuis *et al.*, *Over bomen gesproken* (Baarn 1985), pp. 113–144.
10. Gerhard Liedke, *Im Bauch des Fisches—Ökologische Theologie* (Stuttgart ⁵1988), pp. 39–40.
11. Jürgen Moltmann, *Gott in der Schöpfung* (Munich 1985); Gerhard Liedke, *Im Bauch des Fisches* (Stuttgart 1979); G. Altner, (ed.), *Ökologische Theologie* (Stuttgart 1989).
12. Jürgen Moltmann, *op. cit.*, pp. 281–298.
13. Claus Westermann, *Der Segen in der Bibel und im Handeln der Kirche* (Munich 1968).
14. Sallie McFague, *Models of God* (London 1987), pp. 59–91; Grace Jantzen, *God's World, God's Body* (Philadelphia/London 1984).
15. *Cf.* also, Dorothee Sölle, *To Work and to Love* (Philadelphia 1984); Carter Heyward, *Our Passion for Justice* (New York 1984).
16. *Cf.* Gerda Lerner, *The Creation of Patriarchy* (New York/Oxford 1986). For a comprehensive bibliography see Catharina J. M. Halkes, . . . *En alles zal worden herschapen* (Baarn 1989).
17. Charlene Spretnak and Fritjof Capra, *Green Politics* (Santa Fe, New Mexico 1986).

PART III

Motherhood in Religious Language and Symbolism

Marie-Theres Wacker

God as Mother?: On the Meaning of a Biblical God-symbol for Feminist Theology

MANY MIDDLE-CLASS women in Germany of my mother's generation who went to school before the Second World War, who had to 'dispense with a husband' during the war and the period of reconstruction after it and who married in the early Fifties, have, all their lives, suffered from a conflict decreed by Church and society. They wanted to be good wives and mothers in the Christian sense, but, by reason of the almost exclusive commitment to family and home that this brought about, they were compelled to deny their own lives almost to the point of giving themselves up for lost, or allowing essential aspects of their personality to remain undeveloped. Other possible alternative patterns of living—working as a teacher perhaps, who had of course to remain unmarried, or in the case of Catholic girls, entering a religious order—these were characterised without exception by the ideology of serving and suffering.

But we also have to thank our mothers' generation for women's awakening in the Churches: we daughters can still scarcely imagine how much courage, how much change in ways of thinking, how big a break with truisms this must have meant for these women. Central to their critical inquiry was, from the very beginning, the suspicion that the self-idolising of the masculine, not widely seen as such, in the speaking of (and to) God and the extremely ambivalent estimation and treatment of women, which can often be described as directly sexist, are mutually dependent and become increasingly so. With this critical probe, they began to take a new, close look at the history of the Church(es) and, in particular, to submit the Churches' basic document, the Holy Scriptures, to a re-reading, paying due attention to anything that was anti-feminine. In doing so, the symbol of the God-Mother was also rediscovered. I should like to present this discovery with reference to a text from the Hebrew Bible and, further, to ask how far the symbolising of God as Mother can develop a critically liberating power for women/mothers today, and to ask how far, in this sense, it can be 'glad tidings'. It is a text which, like no other in the Bible, develops the mother image in God's words: chapter 11 of the Book of Hosea[1].

1. Historical-hermeneutical references

The prophet Hosea lived and worked in the eighth century BC, a time characterised by severe external and internal political unrest for Israel. The big powers, Egypt from the West and Assyria from the East, tried alternately to win the territory for themselves and to make Israel a tributary state. The religion promoted by the royal house of the time was directed at the god Baal, the powerful weather and vegetation god, who counted as a kind of divine father of the people and of whom much was hoped for economic and corresponding political well-being. This hope, the prophet Hosea pronounced, was false: he who backed Baal, backed death. Hope lay only in the one God alone who had saved Israel from slavery in Egypt. This theological and, at the same time, political alternative is brought to a head in Chapter 11. We are therefore not dealing in our text in any way with an edifying sermon directed at the mind or the soul of the individual: instead we are launched into the struggle for the true God with its immense political consequences, a conflict which I would unhesitatingly say is *the* real main theme of the Hebrew Bible and which is for me also a central theme of feminist theology.

We must be in no doubt that Hosea's perspective can be said to be frankly androcentric. Throughout the whole prophetic book no woman *herself* speaks, women are merely spoken *about*. But throughout the whole book there is no overly harsh condemnation of women: even at the point when Hosea addresses the blasphemers in feminine symbols, it is men who are meant. That also applies at the level of what is, for Hosea, the central theme, that of the struggle between the gods: certainly we must assume that the god Baal, according to the convictions of the Israelites promoting his cult, did not care for well-being and fruitfulness on his own, but that he needed a goddess in addition. But Hosea makes absolutely no mention of such a goddess; in his view, the struggle takes place between Baal and

JHWH, the true God of Israel. So a man, Hosea, accuses the politically powerful men of his time of deadly, political-religious calculation, a calculation in the name of the masculine god Baal, in action he condemns in the name of his God whom he represents in every way as a likewise masculine God.

A text like this we can perceive as a mirror of our own almost hopelessly patriarchal present. Is that not just our situation: do we not indeed feel ourselves at the mercy of the huge machinery of the patriarchate, maintained by men in political, economic and sexual power, apparently at any price? Is it not so that appalling injustices such as racism and the economic oppression of the Third World by the First were carried out, and are still being carried out, also in the name of the Christian God? Have we women then not really been silenced and robbed of our own state of being ourselves? Seen thus, it may be worthwhile listening to the critical things that the man Hosea has to say to the men of his time.

2. Interpretation

The eleventh chapter of the Book of Hosea is generally celebrated by biblical scholars as the song of God the Father's love for Israel[2]. Helen Schüngel-Straumann, however, the first to decipher it from a feminist theological viewpoint,[3] has correctly pointed out in her interpretation of Hosea 11, that the use of the word 'father' does not occur in this text. Indeed the prophet Hosea never once uses the address 'father' for God, as the Old Testament is, as a whole, very sparing in the use of the father-name for God. Traditional exegesis falls victim here to a false reaction which is in the truest sense patri-archal, when it deduces from the description of Israel as the son of God (11:1) that this God is 'father', and even goes so far, in the proposal of one Scandinavian biblical scholar,[4] as to add the father-title to the wording of Hos. 11:1 by making an 'improvement' to the text.

And yet: the theme of our text is quite clearly a family drama, even if there is no express mention of either father or mother. In verses 1–7 God's care for the young son Israel is described in God's words as follows: 'I called my son out of Egypt, taught him to walk, took him in my arms, raised him to my cheek and fed him.' (*Translator's note*: English language versions do not contain this reference to 'cheek') These activities are, then as now, a mother's everyday activities, and the impression that God's care is being described in maternal images is further strengthened if in verse 3, instead of 'taught to walk', we decide, with Helen Schüngel-Straumann, in favour of the equally possible translation 'quenched his thirst', and in verse

4, instead of 'cheek' we state more precisely 'breast'. But the small boy who had, in the first instance, been granted the means of survival by God's motherly care, turns away to the supposedly powerful Baal who is here contemptuously referred to in the plural with his multitude of images and cults across the land. But in doing so, as the prophet Hosea sees it, Israel conjures up its own political ruin: it is threatened with being crushed between the great powers Assyria and Egypt. And when Israel backs Baal in this political emergency, as is summed up in verse 7, it will be of no use. The alternative is clear: on the side of the supposedly life-giving Baal, death lies in wait; on the side of Hosea's God, stands life. To put it even more clearly: without God the Mother, Israel would have no life at all.

How is it that interpretations of Hosea 11 have, up to now, without exception, still continued to talk of God's fatherly love? One reason could probably lie in the way the Christian Bible-reader looks backward from the New Testament, a look that can only find God the Father in the Hebrew Bible. I can see another reason in the way in which ecclesiastical interpretation has handled such texts: what was important was no longer the world from which the images sprang, rather it was their spiritual meaning that was important, whether that referred to the Church or the individual soul. But feminist theologians, seeking the feminine traces in their tradition, see that the concrete reality from which these images are taken is the world of women, of the mother. They take this discovery literally, as it were, when they stress that Hosea is talking here about God the Mother.

Instead of leaving Israel to the fate for which it is itself to blame, the text goes on, something amazing now happens: God restrains the divine hand, as it were: 'My heart recoils within me,/my compassion (*Translator's note*: German has *Reue*, that is, 'repentance') grows warm and tender./I will not execute my fierce anger.' As the prophet sees it, two emotions, pointing in different directions, both of which can be compared to a glowing fire, are fighting one another here, anger and repentance. Old translations of the text, particularly the Syrian, have instead of 'repentance' (*Reue*), the word for 'mercy' which is the same as that for 'mother's lap' and remind us again of God's maternal dimension. In contrast, anger or rage are clearly characterised as masculine behaviour. In verse 9a of the Hebrew text it says: 'for I am God and not MAN', and that implies, according to the explanatory parallel continuation in verse 9b, that God's holiness does not permit Israel to suffer the anger which a man would vent on his son in a comparable situation. (*Translator's note*: as the author goes on to explain in the following paragraph, the argument is bound up with the German translation of the original by *Mensch*, that is, 'human being', often itself translated as 'man', and not by *Mann*, that is 'man' in its specifically masculine form.)

In commentaries on the Book of Hosea and in editions of the Bible the translation at this decisive point is not 'man' (German: *Mann*) but 'human being' (German: *Mensch*)[5], as if the prophet's words set divine behaviour against general human behaviour. In contrast, I believe with other feminist exegetes that the Hebrew word *isch*, which can indeed also have the general meaning of 'human being', is indeed to be translated at this point in the Book of Hosea by 'man' because that is how Hosea wanted it to be understood. For, in the first part, with its clear description in maternal images of God turning to the little boy Israel, the Hebrew word *adam* is used for 'human being' (*Mensch*) and, in fact, is used to characterise positive human conduct, comparable to God's conduct. God accordingly conducts himself in his loving affection for Israel in a humane way, *i.e.* in a concrete maternal way and he is distinguished from an *isch* by not carrying out his rage and anger. But anger and rage which turn suddenly into destruction, are not only in today's current clichéed sense more masculine modes of conduct, but, in the Book of Hosea, are themselves equated totally with the activities of men in politics and the waging of war. Hosea himself would have accordingly formulated an idea of God in which the maternal activities of tending and nourishing are contrasted with the masculine-destructive emotions and actions. According to this text, the basic analogue of God would therefore not be the masculine-paternal, authoritarian punishment of the 'prodigal son', but maternal caring and feelings of the heart. It is in God that a debate, as it were, takes place between Mother and Father; in God, the Mother can assert herself against the Father for the purpose of saving the son, and the maternal side of God has the last word.

3. Feminist-theological implications

In contrast to the usual patri-archal interpretation of the text, this reminder of a forgotten feminine image of God in the Book of Hosea is already a step forward; but a reminder like this can however emphasise androcentric distortions in the traditional way of speaking of God. Nevertheless we should not adopt the direct and positive inheritance of this feminine image, because the question still remains unanswered as to whether, in doing so, we can go beyond the framework of androcentric distortions in speaking of God. Still, we did at the outset stress that Hosea writes from a clearly androcentric point of view, and in our time also, we should be careful about conservative mother-ideologies as well as those, more recently, of the left. It is certainly not enough now to sing the Divine Mother's unceasing praise because, in doing so, we women are once again, and now even more so, exposed to the danger of being tied to apparently immutable sex-specific clichés, just as if we know what motherliness is: something independent of all social conditions, which can be clearly deduced from the nature *of* woman,[6] and as if therein lies the greatest fulfilment of a woman's life. I am myself the mother of two children and far be it from me to underestimate motherhood and bringing up children. If, however, women are, at the present time, to be committed by the highest ecclesiastical authorities to their role as mother, and if there is fundamentally no readiness to see in women anything other than potential or real mothers, then this is a reduction of women to their biological state which I as a theologian in a country with a fascist past can only view with the greatest disgust.[7]

Three aspects of the text of Hosea 11 above all seem to me noteworthy therefore for a feminist theology.

Nature: Baal is a god whose power Hosea's contemporaries described in comparison with masculine sexual potency, a god who gives the world life with his rain-sperm.[8] In contrast, Hosea summons up God and Mother, but not exactly on the same quasi-genealogical plane: God did not quite *give birth* to the son Israel, instead Israel was *called* from Egypt. It is therefore appropriate to speak here of God's relation with Israel as that of an adoptive parent; it is a question here of a parent-child relationship which does not exactly rest on blood ties. To me, this thought is important in its contrast with an excessively feminist-romantic view of biological motherhood which, onesidedly, takes its bearings from the maternal happiness of well-placed middle-class women in the industrialised countries of the North West corner of the globe. The way we see 'nature' being countered here can, in addition, serve as a critical reminder that the Judaeo-Christian tradition of belief needs to forge other solidarities than those which are merely 'natural growths'.

The personal is political and the political is personal: In Hosea 11 the private, personal sphere and the public, political one are very closely bound together. The unfolding drama of Israel's story with its God, namely as the call from Egypt, the return to Egypt for which Israel itself is responsible and the repeat of the rescue from Egypt, a drama which is set in the conflict of Hosea's time with the great power Assyria, all this is represented in a family story between the mother, the stubborn boy and the father. In this respect, Hosea 11 can be compared with the introductory chapters, Hosea 1–3, which likewise make the family/marriage relationship into a representation of Israel's disturbed relationship with its God and the resulting confusions of politics and cults. On the other hand, the Book of Hosea again and again includes the consequences for the family in its political-theological analyses; here the private is political and the political private. The traditional family ethic of the Church has, up to now, not taken sufficient cognisance of the extent to which this connection is valid for our present time. From a sociological perspective the following is, on the other hand, clear:[9] the societies and economies of the North West industrial countries are based on the unlimited disposability and mobility of individuals and thus question at the deepest level handed-down ways of living, particularly the family. A family ethic which imposes on the partners (and the children) the creation of a private, intact world which, at the same time, reminds women of their natural role as mother and which tries to escape the corruptions of the world outside the family, this ethic is beneath the level of prophetic analyses: the transgressions of the masculine world, Hosea demonstrates (see especially 9: 10–17), are ruinous for mothers and their children, and they also destroy their living space. This really does apply to a frightening degree to many countries in the so-called 'Third World' in which we see the results of impoverishment on a huge scale, brought about by the massive industrialisation imposed by the 'First World' and/or by the expansion of tourism at any price. This separates men from their families as they go in search of the means of survival and, in addition, compels mothers to separate from their children, in so far as the latter do not in any case die off far too early through lack of food, or illness. Here we can no longer say that 'patriarchate' is miscalculating in a naively sex-specific way, rather it is here revealing its rigid hierarchy: women of the First World appear as accomplices in a system which makes a humane life impossible for the men as well as the women and children of the Third World; but even there, in the fight for survival, men are once again given greater chances than women with children and, even more so, the children themselves, particularly the little girls.

God: Mother of mercy: True, Hosea, as we have already stated at the outset, is anything but a 'feminist'; but we find even with him an indication as to how one can move towards taking into account the mother symbol in speaking of God, something which can only serve to stabilise relationships; in doing so, Hosea, in my opinion, reached the limits of patriarchal thinking itself. For Hosea uses the symbol of God-Mother in a peculiarly uneven way. In the reality of his time, as the Book of Hosea presents it, mothers with their children are defenceless victims of masculine destructive mania; the wars under Baal's protection demand them as human victims. In God's words as Hosea presents them, it is precisely the Mother who saves the child in the face of the masculine impulse to destroy. The mother, a silent victim, as the image of God's strength!

But this cannot exactly mean, as has always been preached to Christian women, that *our* strength lies in weakness and humility, this cannot exactly mean establishing pity, mercy and the readiness to achieve reconciliation as typically feminine characteristics which could then be all the more easily exploited in a 'social-cosmetic' way. Rather we must, on the other hand, take this symbol seriously in speaking of *God*.

The mother, a silent victim, as the image of God's strength: for theology, that means that salvation and redemption must not be thought of from the standpoint of power and domination under masculine control, but rather from a position of suffering with, of having compassion for the ever deeper entanglements in which human beings find themselves and where they turn away from God. If God's nature is as the Mother of mercy, then that means that a new beginning, from God's standpoint, is made possible for us without an obligation to retrace our steps, something which we could not achieve anyway. In the symbol of the God-Mother, Hosea broke through the compulsion of always having to speak of God as the powerful one, and the prophet thereby comes very close to the Christian message of the descent of the Son of God to powerlessness, even as far as the Cross. The symbol of the God-Mother preserves the memory of the victims which those who rule demand needlessly, time and again, in order to maintain their rule, the memory of the victims to whom women and children are the first to belong. And so this symbol of the God-Mother counters all attempts to legitimise the rule of human beings over their fellows by appealing to God: but this symbol also makes clear that feminine as well as masculine modes of conduct and qualities cannot just be applied to God in a faithful reflection of our relationships; nor is speaking of God in this way therefore suitable for establishing feminine as well as masculine characteristics; instead it invites us to change reality to correspond to the symbol.

Translated by Gordon Wood

Notes

1. See my interpretation of Hosea 11 in Eva-Renate Schmidt (ed.), *Feministisch Gelesen Bd.2* (Stuttgart 1989), pp. 164–173, as well as my contribution 'Frau—Sexus—Macht. Eine feministisch-theologische Relecture des Hoseabuches' in Marie-Theres Wacker (ed.), *Der Gott der Männer und die Frauen* (Düsseldorf 1987), pp. 101–125.
2. Heinrich Gross in 'Das Hohelied der Liebe Bottes. Zur Theologie von Hos. 11', *Festschrift J. Auer* (Regensburg 1975), pp. 83–91, does indeed speak of Father and Mother in God, but immediately devalues this symbolism by declaring it to be less relevant than the bride symbolism in chapters 1–3 of the Book of Hosea. But on this, for women, disastrous ambivalence, see for example Helgard Balz-Cochois, *Gomer* (Frankfurt 1982).

3. Helen Schüngel-Straumann, 'Gott als Mutter in Hos. 11', *Theol. Quartalschrift* 166 (1986), 119–134 (English translation in *Theology Digest* 1987).

4. Arvid Bruno, *Das Buch der Zwölf* (Stockholm 1957) 33.204.

5. See finally, Jörg Jeremias, 'Der Prophet Hosea', *ATD* 24/1 (new version) (Göttingen 1983) and Alfons Deissler, *Zwölf Propheten: Hosea-Joel-Amos* (Würzburg ²1985). Hans Walter Wolff in *Dodekapropheton 1: Hosea Bibl. Kommentar HIV* (Neukirchen ³1976), does indeed translate with 'man' ('Mann'), but does not evaluate this further in his commentary.

6. On this problem see the penetrating study by Elisabeth Badinter, *Die Mutterliebe. Geschichte eines Gefühls vom 17. Jahrhundert bis heute* (Munich 1984).

7. See Annette Kliewer, '"Von deutscher Gottesmutterschaft". Mütterlichkeit als Maxime "weiblicher" Moral' in Christine Schaumberger (ed.), *Weil wir nicht vergessen wollen . . . zu einer Feministischen Theologie im deutschen Kontext* (Münster 1987), pp. 59–72.

8. This is emphasised by Klaus Koch, *Die Profeten 1. Assyrische Zeit* (Stuttgart 1978), pp. 88–105.

9. See especially, Ulrich Beck, *Risikogesellschaft. Auf dem Weg in eine andere Moderne* (Frankfurt 1986).

Jane Schaberg

The Foremothers and the Mother of Jesus

THE NEW Testament Infancy Narratives are of tremendous significance for any understanding of the image and reality of woman in the West, because they are the source of the Christian Virgin-Mother ideal. These texts have been read traditionally as making a unique claim: that Jesus the Messiah was virginally conceived—that is, that his mother became pregnant solely by the power of divine creativity, and not as a result of sexual intercourse.[1] But have the New Testament texts been properly understood? I think that they have not; in fact they *could* not have been within the confining structures of patriarchal religion.

Reading as a woman reads,[2] and as a reader resisting some aspects of the authors' thought,[3] I propose that Matthew 1:1–15 and Luke 1:20–56; 3:23–38 were originally about an illegitimate conception, not a virginal conception. It was the intention—or better, an intention—of Matthew and of Luke to hand down the tradition they inherited: that Jesus the Messiah had been illegitimately conceived during the period when his mother Mary was betrothed to Joseph. At the pre-gospel stage, this illegitimate conception tradition (probably originating in the circle of the family of Jesus) had already been understood theologically as due in some unexplained way to the power of the Holy Spirit.

Both evangelists worked further with this potentially damaging and potentially liberating material, each developing his own brilliant and cautious presentation. Their caution and their androcentric perspectives, as well as the history of interpretation of the narratives, make this aspect of their meaning difficult to perceive. They took for granted the illegitimacy

112

tradition, of which Christians soon became unaware. In both accounts, Jesus' biological father is absent and unnamed, but adoption by Joseph incorporates the child into the Davidic line. Both evangelists express the faith conviction that in spite of his human origins, the child will be God's, since the Holy Spirit is ultimately responsible for this conception. In both gospels this conviction is presented by depicting an angelic announcement that the pregnancy is divinely ordained. The story of Jesus' illegitimate conception and of his full acceptance as God's child and child of Israel, is the story that anticipates and prepares the reader for the final message of ressurection. The Infancy Narratives attempt as well to initiate the reader into a new framework of social values and realities in the community of the resurrected one, where the last are to be first and the claims of patriarchal power and dominion abolished.

Reading the New Testament narratives in terms of an illegitimate conception, rather than a virginal conception, offers a consistent explanation of many small details. None of the explanations offered here, taken alone, is convincing enough to challenge the traditional interpretation of the Infancy Narratives. But the cumulative effect of these explanations does pose that challenge. There is space here only to examine four elements of the Matthean narrative.[4]

1. The genealogy

Matthew begins his Gospel with the genealogy of Jesus Christ (1:1–17). An unusual feature of this genealogy is the mention of four women: Tamar, Rahab, Ruth, and the wife of Uriah. Why did Matthew choose these particular women as the 'foremothers'? What do they have in common, which may prepared the reader for the story of Mary that follows? A careful look at the stories of the four in the Hebrew Bible shows that their sociological situations are comparable.[5] (1) All four find themselves outside patriarchal family structures: Tamar and Ruth are childless young widows (then Tamar is later pregnant by her father in law); Rahab is a prostitute (if the Rahab in Joshua is the one Matthew is thinking of); Bathsheba is an adulteress and then a widow pregnant with her lover's child. (2) All four are 'wronged' or thwarted by the male world. Without claiming a full feminist consciousness for the authors of these narratives, we can claim an awareness, however dim, that society was patriarchal, and that this caused suffering for women in certain circumstances. (3) In their sexual activity[6] all four risk damage to the social order and their own condemnations. Accusation of improper sexual conduct is actually made in the case of Tamar, implicit in the case of Rahab, avoided in Ruth's case by the secrecy of Boaz, and levelled in Bathsheba's case against her partner. (4) The situations of all four are righted by the actions of men who acknowledge guilt and/or accept responsibility for them, drawing them under patriarchal protection, giving them identity and a future, legitimating them and their children-to-be. The mention of the four women is intended to lead Matthew's reader to expect another story of a woman who becomes a social misfit in some way; is wronged or thwarted; is party to a sexual act which places her in great danger; and whose story has an outcome which repairs the social fabric and ensures the birth of a child who is legitimate or legitimated.

Further, what do these stories of the foremothers have in common theologically, and what is the reader led to expect theologically? The stories show a significant *lack* of miraculous, direct intervention on the part of God, to right the wrongs, or remove the shame, or illuminate the consciousness, or shatter the structures. The stories are instead examples of the divine concealed in and nearly obliterated by human actions, and they share an outlook which stresses God as creator of the context of human freedom. Matthew leads his reader to expect a story which will continue this subtle theologising. It will be a story marked by lack of miraculous, divine intervention, a story rather of divine accommodation to human freedom in the complexity of near-tragedy.

2. The marital and legal situation

In the Palestine of the first century AD, the marriage of a young girl took place in two stages. First came the betrothal, which was a formal exchange in the presence of witnesses of the agreement to marry, and the paying of the bride price. The betrothal constituted a legally ratified marriage, since it began the girl's transfer from her father's power to her husband's, giving the latter legal rights over her, and giving her, for many purposes, the status of a married woman. The betrothal could be broken only by his divorce of her, and any violation by her of his marital 'rights' during this period (when she continued to live in her father's house for about a year) was considered adultery. The second stage was the marriage proper, the transfer of the girl to her husband's home where he assumed her support. Only at this point did she definitely pass into her husband's power. It was normally assumed that the girl was a virgin at the time of her betrothal, and, at least in Galilee, also at the time of her completed marriage.

In Matthew 1:18–25, Mary is described as having been found pregnant in the period between the betrothal and the completed marriage, before she and Joseph 'came together', probably meaning before Mary was brought to Joseph's home. Joseph's reaction in v. 19 makes it plain that he is not responsible for the pregnancy (and v. 25 will underline this). Adultery or rape are two normal ways Joseph has of explaining the pregnancy with which he is confronted. The case of a betrothed virgin's sexual intercourse with someone other than her husband during the period of bethrothal is handled in the Hebrew Bible only in Deuteronomy 22:23–27, the text many scholars think is alluded to by both evangelists.

If there is a betrothed virgin (MT *nă 'ărā bĕtûlâ*; LXX: *pais parthenos*) and a man meets her in the city, and lies with her, then you shall bring them both out to the gate of that city, and you shall stone them to death with stones, the young woman because she did not cry for help, though she was in the city, and the man because he violated his neighbor's wife; so you shall purge the evil from the midst of you.[7] But if in the open country a man meets young woman who is betrothed, and the man seizes her and lies with her, then only the man who lay with her shall die. But to the young woman you shall do nothing; in the young woman there is no offence punishable by death, for this case is like that of a man attacking and murdering his neighbour; because he came upon her in the open country and though the betrothed young woman cried for help there was no one to rescue her.

It is important that we try to determine as far as possible how this law was applied in Matthew's time, and the range of options that would be presented in such a case as he describes, involving pregnancy. (1) There is evidence that in a hearing before a judge or judges there would be an effort to go beyond Deuteronomy and not make everything turn on the scene of the act. For example, according to Philo, it had to be questioned whether she cried out and resisted, or co-operated willingly, or even whether she *could* cry out and resist, or was gagged and bound, overcome by superior strength, and whether the man had accomplices.[8] (2) There is evidence also of a less severe legal system in the first century, according to which the death penalty would not be enforced for an adulteress, but divorce was probably obligatory. (3) There may have existed in some circles as well a rigorous *halakah* which required the layman (as well as the priest) to divorce even a raped woman; under a less severe *halakah*, divorce of the raped woman by the layman was not obligatory but probably allowed. (4) If no hearing was held, the woman may have been presumed guilty, and divorce would be the outcome, possibly on trivial grounds. (5) Concerning the fate of children of an adulteress, Sirach 23:22–26 contains harsh words: her cursed memory and disgrace live on in them (*cf.* Wisdom 3:16–19), and punishment falls on them (perhaps the assembly's decision that they are illegitimate, and the husband's rejection of them as his heirs). They are

piously wished premature deaths and sterile unions. We can suspect that
the children of raped women or women only suspected of adultery were
also such social misfits. (6) Finally, let me mention what has been called
'the humane provision of Israel's regulations concerning adoption': the
ruling principle was that any male child accepted under the rule of the
head of a family was considered his son in all respects.[9]

In Matthew's opening lesson on righteousness and Torah, Joseph, 'a just
man' (that is, Torah-observant), and unwilling to expose his wife to public
disgrace, 'resolved to divorce her quietly' (1:19). The logic of the story[10]
indicates that Joseph felt himself obligated, or allowed, to divorce rather
than complete the marriage. I take this to mean that he ruled out the
hearing to determine whether Mary had been seduced or raped, thus
shielding her (and himself) from public shame and questioning, from the
possibility of conviction on the charge of adultery, with its most likely
punishment of a degrading divorce, attendant indignities and bleak future,
and perhaps from the reasonable likelihood that rape could not be proven.

The angelic message in verses 20–21, however, urges the hometaking, the
completion of the marriage. 'Joseph, son of David, do not be afraid to take
Mary your wife into your home, for the child begotten in her is through
the Holy Spirit.' One critic comments, 'The angel, by removing the
suspicion of adultery and of violence, makes Mary acceptable to her
husband.'[11] In my judgment, hometaking would remove the suspicion of
adultery; a Torah-observant man would probably not complete the
marriage with an adulteress. But the home-taking would *not* remove the
suspicion of rape: A Torah-observant layman, following the *halakah* that
allowed him to marry a raped woman, could procede with the marriage.
Since in his Gospel Matthew insists that the Torah is valid and must be
interpreted without relaxation (5:18–19), on the hermeneutical principle of
the priority of the love command, we can say he intends the angelic solution
to the dilemma to be a righteous and legal one. It is as well the most
merciful alternative offered by the Law. Joseph, accepting the pregnant
Mary into his home accepts responsibility for the child she is carrying. The
words to Joseph in 1:21, 'You will call his name Jesus', are equivalent to a
formula of adoption. Joseph, by exercising the father's right to name the
child, acknowledges Jesus and thus becomes his adoptive and legal father.

3. The role of the Holy Spirit

What does Matthew mean when he says in verse 18 that Mary was found
pregnant 'through the Holy Spirit', and in verse 20 that 'the child begotten
in her is through the Holy Spirit'? Few modern critics think that these

verses refer to anything but a virginal conception, a counter-explanation to human paternity. It is rapidly becoming a scholarly consensus, however, that the idea of a virginal conception is found nowhere but in the two New Testament Infancy Narratives, and that there are no real parallels in the Hebrew or Greek Bible, in intertestamental literature, or in the Pauline or Johannine writings; nor is the idea alluded to anywhere else in the New Testament. Critics generally agree that there are no real pagan parallels either, since pagan myths consistently involve a type of *hieros gamos* or divine marriage, with pregnancy resulting from sexual penetration of some sort.[12] My suggestion for reading Matthew is a simple one: since nothing in the context of Matthew 1 requires us to read the phrases in terms of a virginal conception, they should be read against the wider Jewish and Christian background. This means they should be read in a figurative or symbolic sense.

In all the relevant Jewish and New Testament literature, divine begetting presupposes and does not replace human parenting. There are texts that speak of divine begetting to stress that God's power is the ultimate source of human life and generation, or to stress that God sometimes communicates a special spiritual dimension of life to humans, over and above or within human existence. In this latter sense Paul and John speak of the Christian begotten by the Spirit or by God.

In the light of these texts, Matt. 1:18, 20 can be read to mean that the Holy Spirit empowers this birth as all births are divinely empowered, that this child's existence is willed by God, that God is the ultimate power of life behind and in this as in all conceptions. My sense is that Matthew means more than—but not less than—this. In the situation he has described, this dimension of meaning is extremely significant: this child's existence is not an accident or mistake, and is not cursed. But Matthew is also clearly speaking about the election of this child from the womb for a role in Israel's history: Jesus will save his people from their sins (1:21), and will be called Emmanuel (1:23). Further, this begetting constitutes him Son of God in a special sense, as the one who sums up in his existence the whole history of Israel. Jesus is begotten through the Holy Spirit in his human paternity; he is one with God from his conception.

4. Isaiah 7:14

Between the angel's words to Joseph and Joseph's obedience to those words, Matthew inserts his first fulfillment citation: 'All this took place to fulfill what the Lord had spoken by the prophet: "Behold, the virgin (*parthenos*) will conceive and will give birth to a son and they will call his name

Emmanuel."' The sign offered by Isaiah to King Ahaz during the Syro-Ephraimite war in the eighth century BC was the imminent birth of a child naturally conceived, who would signal God's presence and care for Judah. The Greek translation of Isaiah's Hebrew 'almâ (young woman) by parthenos (virgin) does not indicate a miraculous conception. Rather, the Greek translator simply meant that one who is now a virgin will conceive by natural means. Matthew himself added the citation to a pre-existing narrative or body of infancy tradition.

But why, of all the texts available to him, did Matthew choose this one to elucidate and support his story of the origins of Jesus? I think it is likely that the word parthenos played a role in his choice. But Matthew was not thinking of a virgin conceiving miraculously, but of the law in Deuteronomy 22:23–27 concerning the seduction or rape of a betrothed virgin, the law he presupposes in his presentation of the dilemma of Joseph. Although he does not quote the law, this is the catchword association that triggered his use of Isaiah 7:14. This would mean that he understood the text as the Greek translator did, referring to one who was a virgin and who conceived naturally. The placement of the citation underscores the way the divine assurance overturns Joseph's decision to divorce Mary.

The problem before Matthew was to make theological sense of a tradition concerning the illegitimate pregnancy. If we pause for a minute and ask what texts and traditions were available to him to be used for such a purpose, we find that none would be clear and unambiguous choices. No text in the Hebrew Bible I can think of fully vindicates a wronged woman who has been seduced or raped, or legitimates the child born of such a union—much less prepares for the startling thought that this might be the origin of the expected Messiah. There were, in fact, no texts and traditions ready at hand for such a theological task. Matthew had to create out of fragments easily misunderstood, and one of these is Isaiah 7:14.

The virgin betrothed and seduced or raped is, then, in the great Matthean paradox, the virgin who conceives and bears the child they will call Emmanuel. His origin is ignominious and tragic, but Matthew's point is that his existence is divinely willed; his messiahship was not negated by the way he was conceived. The wording in which the NT conception story survives is 'when scrutinized closely, curious and equivocal'.[13] This is due not to the desire to be enigmatic, nor to the stress and strain of presenting a novel notion of divine begetting without human paternity (a virginal conception). It is due rather to something more difficult: the effort to be honest, discreet and profound, dealing with material that resisted—and still resists—the theologian's art: the siding of God with the outcast, endangered woman and child.

5. Conclusion and response

In this interpretation of Matthew 1, God 'acts' in a radically new way, outside the patriarchal norm but within the natural event of human conception. The story of the illegitimacy of Jesus supports the claim Luke makes, that Mary represents the oppressed who have been liberated. But Matthew's version, with its focus on Joseph, is androcentric, primarily about and for males; it does not confront the causes or structures of oppression. It is not the story of the mother of Jesus. By linking her story, however, with those of the four women listed in the genealogy, Matthew implies that salvation history is not essentially a male enterprise. We can carry that implication further to challenge our deepest prejudices and presuppositions, by breaking the silence of the Silent Night.

Notes

1. See R. E. Brown, *The Birth of the Messiah* (Garden City 1977); J. A. Fitzmyer, *The Gospel According to Luke I–IX* (Garden City 1981).
2. The hope is that this reading will bring us closer to a more inclusive human reading.
3. See J. Fetterly, *The Resisting Reader* (Bloomington 1978); *The New Feminist Criticism*, ed. E. Showalter (New York 1985).
4. My book, *The Illegitimacy of Jesus* (San Francisco 1987), includes further discussion of Matthew 1, treatment of the Lukan Infancy Narrative, of the pre- and post-gospel illegitimacy tradition, and discussion of the feminist implications of my reading.
5. See Susan Niditch, 'The Wronged Woman Righted', *Harvard Theological Review* 72 (1979), pp. 143–49.
6. Or in Ruth's case, perhaps only suspicion of sexual activity (see the commentaries on Ruth 3:4, 7–9, 12–13).
7. The commentaries refer to this case as 'seduction': the man 'seizes' the virgin who does not resist; this is considered adultery on the part of both.
8. Philo, *Spec. Led.* 3. 77–78.
9. C. Tchernowitz, 'The Inheritance of Illegitimate Children According to Jewish Law', *Jewish Studies in Memory of Israel Abrahams*, ed. G. A. Kohut (New York 1927), pp. 402–403.
10. The phrase about the Holy Spirit in v. 18 is read by most critics as an aside to the reader.
11. A. Tosato, 'Joseph, Being a Just Man', *Catholic Biblical Quarterly* 41 (1979), p. 551.
12. See R. E. Brown, *The Virginal Conception and Bodily Resurrection of Jesus* (New York 1973).
13. G. Vermes, *Jesus the Jew* (New York 1973), p. 221.

Els Maeckelberghe

'Mary': Maternal Friend or Virgin Mother?

The highest stage of honour
that a woman has ever reached is your most empty stage.
They stand so deep below—
from the beginning of the world,
until the last day.
There is not one
    who can achieve your praise or fame.

1. 'Mary': The product of a tug of war lasting centuries

MARY—WHO is she really? An astonishing number of ideas about her have accumulated in Europe. She is the Lady of the mediaeval monk. She is also the Mother of the Seven Dolours, pierced by seven swords. The plaster statue in the grotto at Massabielle in Lourdes is another representation of Mary, as is also the black Madonna of Czestochowa. Going beyond Europe too, Mary is present in many different forms. Both in time and geographically, she has many different meanings. Is she perhaps really the raped goddess that some people want to make her today? Or is she the young woman singing the Magnificat? It is a complete illusion to think that you have a clearly defined figure if you just pronounce the name 'Mary'. Many different cargoes sail under the flag 'Mary'.[1] It is a very flexible name that can be adapted to the needs of the time when and the place where it is invoked.

To express this more precisely, people have again and again seen in 'Mary' characteristics that have been appropriate at that particular time and in that particular culture. There are, however, two characteristics that

120

seem to have been constant, although they have not always been prominently present: 'Mary' is a virgin and 'Mary' is a mother. Virginity and motherhood form the chorus in the background of the melodies that are composed and sung about 'Mary'. The question forming the point of departure for what follows is this: What is the place and the significance of the virginity and the motherhood of 'Mary' in a culture that has has been coloured by the Roman Catholic Church?

I would like to discuss two methodological approaches that might lead to an explanation of the phenomenon of 'Mary' and the psychological effect of that phenomenon in a celibate clerical culture. The first of these methodological approaches is based on the distinction noted by A. Rich in connection with motherhood between institution and the world of human experience. The second is an analysis that is specifically sexual. This means that what is investigated is what the institution 'Mary' has to say with regard to women, as distinct from what it has to say with regard to men. The same also applies to the level of human experience. In other words, how do women experience 'Mary' and how do men experience 'Mary'?

The distinction made by Rich between institution and the level of experience is essential with regard to 'Mary'. Up till now, research in connection with 'Mary' has all too frequently taken as its point of departure interpretations formulated by higher authorities. It has been assumed, for example, in a very simplistic way, that the official standpoint has also been the universally accepted one.[2] It is not so easy to discover precisely what was initiated with the institutional 'Mary' at the level of human experience and how 'Mary' brings women in contact with who they really are. Finding the 'Mary' who moved people of flesh and blood is certainly not an easy task. 'One must find isolated words, isolated images: one must travel the road of metaphor, of icon, to come back to the figure who has moved the hearts of men and women and abides shining, worthy of our love, compelling it.'[3]

At the level of experience, we have to take the recipient into account. People who are confronted with the institutional 'Mary' are not an empty vessel into which this image disappears unconditionally and unaltered and is then absorbed. The line between the message and the recipient is not straight. It is possible for surprises to occur on the side of the recipient. The message is interpreted and modelled by the creativity of the recipient.[4] Those who receive the message, the images, are women and men. The fact that we enter the world as a girl or as a boy determines our being in the world and how we look at things. Expressed simplistically and almost as a caricature, it can be said that the sight of a car evokes for a boy dreams of speed, strength and manhood, whereas for a girl it means first and foremost the possibility of a change of place. The way in which 'Mary' is seen and interpreted is determined by whether it is a girl or a boy looking at it.

I believe that the institution and the level of experience with regard to 'Mary' are much closer to each other in the case of men than in that of women, and that 'Mary's' virginity is especially important for men, whereas her motherhood is the point of contact for women.

2. 'Mary': The canalization of sexual desires?

In his book, *The Cult of the Virgin Mary*,[5] M. P. Carroll attempts to discover the origin of the Marian devotion. The most plausible explanation is, in his opinion, provided by psycho-analysis. I shall present Carroll's line of thought here* without considering the plausibility of his theory with regard to the development of male identity. His point of departure is the observation that sons, who are brought up in a family in which the father figure is not present in a sufficiently pronounced way, have a strong tendency to cling sexually to their mothers. This leads to uncertainty with regard to their maleness and causes an exaggeratedly male behaviour. Sexual desire for the mother has to be suppressed. This in turn gives rise to the Marian devotion.

Carroll's first hypothesis is that a fervent devotion to Mary on the part of men is a practice that men—who are characterised by a violent, but also powerfully suppressed sexual desire for their mothers—admit in order to assimilate this surplus of sexual energy in an acceptable manner[6].

Carroll's second hypothesis is that, throughout the centuries, form has been given to the various characteristics of the Marian devotion by this violent, but at the same time powerfully suppressed desire on the part of the son for his mother. The emphasis on the virginity of 'Mary' is therefore not purely fortuitous. If Mary had been simply a mother, the son's sexual desire for his mother would have been only too clear in the Marian devotion. Mary's virginity, however, has served to conceal this[7] 'Mary' must be and stay a virgin, so that she can continue to be the pleasure garden for male fantasies. 'Mary' may not be associated with sexuality. If this is, however, the case, then this beautiful construction that serves to canalize male sexual fantasies collapses at once.

These are two working hypotheses providing clarification in the case of a number of remarkable phenomena in the history of 'Mary'. Carroll demonstrates the way in which his hypotheses explain the remarkable connection in the fifth century of the sudden appearance of the Marian devotion, the emphasis on Christ's suffering and the insistence, which, as it were, emerged from nowhere, on the celibacy of the clergy[8]. It is open to question, of course, whether these hypotheses really prove the value of the claims that Carroll makes for them, that is, whether they provide an explanation for the emergence of the cult of Mary. They do, however, certainly help to explain why, for example, a whole chapter could be written without any great problems in a nineteenth-century devotional book on 'the most holy breasts of Mary'—a chapter, in which Jesus asks his mother 'with little coaxing glances' to give him her breast to suck[9].

Hans Urs von Balthasar's statement about the 'Marian origin of the grace of celibacy'[10] can also be seen in an entirely different light when seen in this perspective. So too can the following quotation from another frequently reprinted book on 'Our Lady to the Church's priests, her dearly beloved sons': 'Wash yourselves in this source so that you may become more and more pure. Your immaculate Mother, dearly beloved sons, covers you with her heavenly cloak and she will gently help you to experience the virtue of purity'.[11] It is not necessary to be a Freudian to recognise the highly charged sexual content of these statements.

The question that arises here, then, for women, is clearly: How is it that they feel attracted to the cult of Mary? Carroll insists that a strong sense of identification with the Virgin Mary gives a woman the opportunity to fulfil in substitution her desire for sexual contact with her father. It also gives her the opportunity to realise her longing for a baby from her father via a substitute[12].

I would argue here that this third hypothesis takes Carroll into a very obscure zone. He continues to insist on a close parallel between the development of boys and that of girls in the oedipal phase. Not only boys, but also girls, he says, experience this stage of development. Anyone who remains within this framework of thought is bound to formulate this third hypothesis. The strongest emphasis is placed here on the oedipal crisis.

Feminist psychologies have, on the other hand, made it quite obvious that a feeling of continuity is very important for girls. Chodorow, for example, has pointed out with great emphasis that the bond with the mother occurs both in the case of girls and in that of boys, but that it is different in kind in each case. Boys are orientated towards sexual differences and towards the triangular relationship with the father. Girls, on the other hand, remain much longer orientated only towards the mother and persist with this relationship of two persons. The oedipal crisis does not have the same degree of radicality for girls as for boys. No change takes place in girls in which they turn away from their mother and towards their father. In the case of girls, the diadic (mother-daughter) relationship is extended into a triadic (mother-daughter-father) structure. Identification with the mother is also more central in the case of girls than in that of boys. Carroll has clearly sensed something here in affirming that boys do not identify themselves with their mother, but cling to her sexually.[13]. He has, however, elaborated this idea exclusively in the case of the man. Unfortunately, he has not dealt with the consequences for the woman's development.

His observation that the girl's identification with her mother is not interrupted is important for the relationship between women and 'Mary'. Mary's attractiveness for women can only be understood in the light of this idea of identification. For women, 'Mary' is not experienced as over and against, but in continuity with herself. The consequence of this is that 'Mary' is not an object of sexual fantasies, but a subject with which women can identify.

Even at the institutional level, something of these differences has been sensed, if only with a negative effect. The nineteenth-century poem quoted in translation at the beginning of this article expresses particularly well the tenor of the relationship that has existed between 'Mary' and 'ordinary' women. What it says in fact is that women have to identify with 'Mary', but, whatever they do in whatever way they lead their lives, they will never succeed in approaching 'Mary', let along in equalling her. A relationship of this kind is certainly not present in the case of men. For women, 'Mary' is clearly an identification figure whom they have to take as an example. The ultimate goal of being a woman is to become like 'Mary', even if it is impossible to achieve it. With regard to women, the resemblance with 'Mary' is emphasised: 'Mary' and all women have their sex in common. With regard to men, on the other hand, the situation is quite different: 'Mary' is, for men, the other who does not resemble the man, with the result that she is not an identification figure. For men, 'Mary' is someone who is over and against them.

There are several striking examples of the difference in the meaning that 'Mary' has for women on the one hand and for men on the other to be found in the nineteenth-century devotional literature. It was, for instance, possible for a book to be written which was entirely addressed to 'my dearly beloved sons'—'Mary' is speaking to male readers here—and this is successful until the chapter on chastity is reached. At this point, 'Mary' abruptly begins to address her daughters quite explicitly. But is this just by chance?

It is difficult to understand how women can identify with this 'Mary', who has been described by so many as 'suppressive'. The fact that it is impossible to achieve this identification is clear from the examples given. But here we have to turn once again to Rich's distinction between institution and the level of experience. 'Mary' is, for women, always someone who is different from what the official statements and ideas might at first sight lead us to suspect. It is clear from conversations with women that—if they attribute any place at all to 'Mary'—they see her above all as 'that woman with the difficult son'. Women see 'Mary' first and foremost as a woman and not as an exceptional being who is said to be both virgin and mother at the same time.[14] 'Mary' is, in other words, not someone to whom they can turn to as someone who is over and against them, but someone with whom that can speak as an equal, someone who knows their own difficulties and especially those involved in the bringing up of children who go their own way. 'Mary' is someone who resembles these women, someone who has experienced all that they have experienced and can therefore offer advice as a kind of maternal friend.

Another meaning that 'Mary' has is that of the protective woman. A contemporary example of this can be found in Margaret Atwood's *Cat's Eye*.[15] The main character in this novel, Elaine, looks back at her childhood and at the cruelties she suffered. The first half of the book closes with a test which Elaine has to undergo. She is forced to descend into a ravine and finds that she cannot get out. She hears a voice and sees a human figure. 'You can go home now', she says. 'Everything is OK. Go home.'

Although she did not have a religious upbringing, Elaine can only call this figure by her name: Mary. When the figure disappears, Elaine says: 'She is still with me, invisible, wrapping me in warmth and painlessness. She heard me despite everything.' Shortly afterwards, Elaine's mother finds her and Elaine says that this figure was the 'Virgin Mary'.

We should not be led astray by the word 'virgin' here. Elaine uses the terms that have been offered to her by the culture that surrounds her. In the story, however, the term 'virgin' plays no part—or at least it does not have the narrowly sexual definition of what virginity means. It is not by chance that the apparition of Mary in the middle of this book is described as a kind of pivot—the figure appearing to Elaine is at the same time both the mother for whom she is longing and the mother she herself would like to be, in other words, a protective woman. The apparition is an identification figure, both for Elaine herself and for her mother.

We can sum up and say, then, that, at the institutional level, there is a twofold division. For men, 'Mary' is an object to whom they turn, whereas, for women, she is an identification figure, a figure whom they have to take as an example. At this institutional level, virginity is extremely important. 'Virginity'; qualifies every statement about 'Mary'. For men, 'Mary' is an object to whom they can turn because she is the virgin mother. For women, she is a virginal example, especially as far as her chastity is concerned. This chastity is both expressed in the sphere of the body and is also visible in everything that she does. In this way, despite her influential presence, 'Mary' always remains tidily one step below the Trinity. She never tries to seize hold of power.

At the level of experience too, the same twofold division exists. For men, the level of experience seems to be nicely in agreement with the institutional level. 'Mary' is an object and the emphasis on her virginity enhances her position as an object. For women, on the other hand, 'Mary' may certainly be an identification figure, but for reasons that are quite different from those that obtain at the institutional level.

3. 'Mary': The maternal friend?

The two methodological approaches that I have outlined provide a clear and subtly-shaded image of the psychological meaning that 'Mary' has for women and for men. For men, 'Mary' is above all an object that can be filled with all kinds of fantasies. In itself, this does not seem to be very problematical—fantasies have to be expressed in one way or another. But it is not quite as simple as that. The image that men have of 'Mary' has become normative and it is held up to women as an example. It has been painted by a patriarchal, white, heterosexual, Western, celibate, male hand. As long as this man wants to go on being himself, 'Mary' will continue to be necessary as an object.

Listening to what women have to say about 'Mary' implies a radical change. The image that they paint leaves little space for the exclusive place that 'Mary' has occupied until now. As long as patriarchal, white, heterosexual, Western, celibate man fails to recognise that 'Mary' should not be made into an object, she will continue to be the plaything of fantasies.

Let us allow 'Mary' to become once again a woman in the past of whom we know very little. Let us listen to women of today. The institution will only have something positive to say to women if their world of experience is on offer. Stepping outside the vicious celibate circle can only take place if women are taken seriously as the hermeneutical centre of interpretation of being the Church today.[16] 'Mary' will then become one of the many 'women friends' taking part in the conversation that is conducted by the community of believers today.

Translated by David Smith

Notes

1. In order to show that Mary does not refer to a single fixed content, I have written the name as 'Mary'.
2. There is little indication, for example, in a book that is otherwise very well worth reading, M. Warner's *Alone of All Her Sex. The Myth and the Cult of the Virgin Mary* (London 1976), of any reflection about how certain images of 'Mary' have been received. The author remains throughout at the institutional level.
3. See Mary Gordon, in L. Cunningham, *Mother of God* (1982), p. 12.
4. The collection *Immaculate and Powerful* was conceived around this idea, namely that religious symbols form both the elements of the suppression of women and also the opportunity leading to a creative elaboration. See C. W. Atkinson, C. H. Buchanan and M. R. Miles, eds., *Immaculate and Powerful. The Female in Sacred Image and Social Reality* (Boston 1985), pp. 1–14. In this article, I emphasise the possibility of a positive interpretation of images by women. I would not deny, however, that 'Mary' can also be a very suppressive image.
5. M. P. Carroll, *The Cult of the Virgin Mary* (Princeton 1986).
6. *Ibid.*, p. 56.
7. *Ibid.*, p. 59.
8. *Ibid.*, pp. 75–89.
9. *De Lof Van Maria* (1855), pp. 87–91.
10. H. U. von Balthasar, *Maria nu* (Bonheiden 1988), pp. 28–31 (German original: *Maria für heute*, Freiburg).
11. This book is an edition published by the Marian priests' movement and contains 'messages from Mary to priests, mediated by Father Stefano Gobbi'.
12. Carroll, *op. cit.*, p. 59.
13. *Ibid.*, p. 53.
14. I would not deny that the institutional level influences and determines the world of women's experience. But being aware of this is not the end—despite the restrictions imposed by the institutional level, there is still the possibility of creative elaboration.
15. M. Atwood, *Cat's Eye* (Toronto 1988).
16. For the meaning of this term, see E. Schüssler Fiorenza, *Bread Not Stone. The Challenge of Feminist Biblical Interpretation* (Boston 1984).

Ursula King

The Divine as Mother

God is love,
and for love of us has become woman.
The ineffable being of the Father has out of compassion
with us become mother.
By loving, the Father has become woman.

Clement of Alexandria (+ 215)

O Mother! Thou art present in every form;
Thou art in the entire universe and in its tiniest
and most trifling things.
Wherever I go and wherever I look,
I see Thee, Mother, present in thy cosmic form.
The whole world—earth, water, fire and air—
All are thy forms, O Mother, the whole world of
birth and death.

Ramprasad (Hindu saint, 18th century)

(Some) believe that to call God 'Mother' would be illegitimate, and cause
hurt . . . (Others) believe that they have heard it said in the Word of God
that the Father of our Lord Jesus Christ, the Maker of us all, resembles,
though he far transcends, everything that is best in the female way of being
human and the human way of being motherly.

Alan E. Lewis, ed., *The Motherhood of God* (1984) pp. 65, 66.

THE FIRST two quotations are an example of how, in the language of devotion and prayer, the Divine has been invoked as 'Mother', associated with the experience of love and compassion, of life and death, of an assuring presence pervading the whole world. The third, more recent example expresses clearly how contemporary Christians are divided over calling God 'Mother' because it has been the dominant practice in the Christian tradition to address God as 'Father'. However, the almost exclusive use of this metaphor has become problematic and is much questioned today, not only by feminists. We have to ask ourselves how far the use of 'Father' for describing divine reality is a root metaphor we cannot do without in Christianity or whether it can be considerably widened out and enriched through thinking and speaking of God also as 'Mother'.

We can find many examples of motherly qualities and activities associated with God in the language of the Bible and Christian tradition, yet these have always remained rather marginal in a predominantly patriarchal Church with strong androcentric forms of thought. But we do possess alternative sources of experience and vision in the Christian tradition for calling God 'Mother', too little reflected upon so far. It is important to uncover these perspectives and make them more central, but also to look for further, complementary insights in religious traditions outside Christianity.

1. Some clarifications

The enquiry into divine motherhood is undertaken from the critical perspective of contemporary consciousness which examines the resources of the past anew and brings to them new questions arising from new experiences where old certainties can no longer be taken for granted. Philosophers and theologians often debate the existence of God which is more problematic than ever today. To be a person of faith, to believe in and be empowered by God's presence and all-transforming spirit, demands courage and humility in an age of uncertainty and unreason. The existential, philosophical and theological problems pertaining to our experience and understanding of God are further compounded by the frequent association of God with the image of the father, an image far too impoverished and constraining for many of our contemporaries. This raises the question what we might gain by calling God 'Mother', what the mother image implies in terms of a new and richer disclosure of meaning, and how far it may again be problematic for our understanding of God and ourselves, although posing different problems from those associated with the father image.

I would like to make it clear that three considerations have guided my choice of material for this brief article. Most articles in this volume of *Concilium* deal with Christianity, but in a discussion of divine motherhood it is both helpful and necessary to draw inspiration from the immense resources of global religious symbolism and thought. However, within the present limits it is impossible to undertake a wide comparative survey and describe a great range of historical examples concerning divine motherhood. I have ᴢefore firstly chosen to restrict my discussion to some examples from Hinduism which is exceptionally rich in divine female imagery and symbolism.

Secondly, naming God is for the Christian linked to God's own Word, to God having spoken first through particular events and especially through the person of Jesus. Divine speaking is thus linked to and limited by specific historic forms which are both revelatory and obscuring, for they can never disclose all of divine reality and being. Thus we must always remain aware that our image, symbols and concepts are in one way or another human constructs about Ultimate Reality and not the Divine in Itself. The categories of our historically circumscribed language and thought forms try to express the experience and understanding of an all-encompassing reality of the Divine, Something/One far transcending what we can ever be of know, but also Something/One immanent, a ground and source of all being, life and creation. I shall speak of the 'Divine' rather than 'God' in most of what follows, not only in order to overcome the personal/impersonal dichotomy, but also to get away from the 'God-the-father' association and the polarity God/Goddess which many people pose.

An important third consideration concerns the necessary distinction between the rich female symbolism of the Divine, found in many religions and often anthropomorphically represented as the Goddess, and the frequently associated, but separate idea of divine motherhood. I shall only deal with the latter which is a more limited topic as not every goddess is necessarily a mother goddess. The realm of divine female imagery and symbolism is larger than the idea of motherhood, just as woman's experience is not coterminous and identical with human motherhood – it is a central but not exclusive aspect of her life.

2. Divine motherhood in Hinduism

The idea of divine motherhood has a long tradition in Hinduism and finds expression at many different levels. It is an immensely rich and rewarding theme whose origin goes back to ancient times, for already in the Mohenjodaro civilisation various figurines are found representing the

Great Mother or Nature Goddess, and ancient texts allude to a mother of all created beings, sometimes perceived as 'Mother Earth' or later as 'Great Mother' who is a World-Mother or Mother of the Universe. These epithets are particularly associated with the *Devi*, the Great Indian Goddess, ultimately understood as a metaphysical principle of Oneness known in innumerable shapes and forms and unassailable in her power. In the mythology of the Great Goddess the idea of motherhood is less directly linked with having children, with giving physical birth, than with the more universal idea of the origin of all life and of the world as a whole: She is the source of everything, of the earth, of plants, of animals, of human beings, and She has the power to nurture and sustain them all and thereby guarantee their continuity.

In the realm of nature there is the idea that rivers, in fact the whole geography of India, are sacred and imbued with motherly qualities. Reverence is given above all to the Ganges whose most popular epithet is 'Mother Ganges' – *Ganga Ma* – and the country itself is spoken of as 'Mother India' – *Bharat Mata*. Many particular goddesses are called 'Mother', such as Ambika, widely worshipped by Gujaratis, or Annapurna, said to be 'the one who feeds' or is 'full of food'. She is celebrated for her power of sustaining life by giving food, just as a mother does, and her nurture can be understood in both a physical and spiritual sense. Saraswati, the goddess of wisdom, depicted with a palm leaf manuscript in her hand, is said to be 'the mother of the Vedas', the foundational scriptures of Hinduism. Saraswati represents wisdom in teaching and grants talent in writing and eloquence in speech; here the mental and spiritual aspects of nurture and sustenance are prominent.

A very powerful Indian idea is that of *Shakti*, the primal divine energy always represented as female and without which no male god can act. *Shakti* is the dynamic power which reverberates through the entire universe and makes everything alive. Invoked by many names and represented in many different forms, *Shakti* is also the 'Great Mother', the Indian *Magna Mater*, who represents the supreme essence of the universal Goddess. She is not only the primal womb and ground of life, but she also reveals the tender, gentle, comforting, reassuring, 'motherly' dimensions of the Divine in whom devotees seek refuge in their confusion and helplessness. She alleviates their anguish, protects them from all evil and removes their suffering. Thus the ultimate saving reality is here seen as Mother. This doctrine and worship of divine motherhood attained its culmination in India among the *Shaktas*, the followers of *Shakti* who have their own religious practices and scriptures. By invoking her saving grace the devotees see 'the mother of the whole world' in the following terms, as described by an Indian writer:

Thus, the one, infinite, uncreated, transcendent and omni-present God-the-Mother is kindness incarnate. She is merciful, tender nourisher and protectress, particularly of her erring children who worship her. The Divine Mother of the universe manifests—incarnates—herself on difficult occasions in order to help. She abides in all beings as a mother who is both benign and fearful. So, she is *coincidentia oppositorum*: all contradictions merge in her, that is, she transcends everything. (Madtha 1980, p. 183).

This text alludes to the fact that the Divine Mother is not all goodness and sweetness. She is both beautiful and terrifying, benign and malevolent, for she not only personifies the origin of life but also that of death and disease. This polarity is strongly visible in the female village deities of popular Hinduism with their ambivalent nature and unpredictable moods. They possess the contrasting role of guarding the village on one hand and being the source of disease and sudden death on the other, thus threatening the village's stability and existence. There is even a group of goddesses, usually seven, sometimes eight or even sixteen, who are always perceived together and jointly addressed as 'Mothers' but whose nature is entirely malevolent, dangerous, wild and bloodthirsty. They represent violent, untamed forces and are especially associated with diseases, particularly those affecting children.

Nowhere is the polarity of the ambivalent goddess symbolism more apparent than in the goddess Kali, primarily at home in Bengal but widely worshipped all over India. She has a long and complex history yet she grew to ever larger stature to become the Mother of all. Her cult grew not only through *Shakti* worshippers in Bengal, but especially through the fervent devotion of Ramprasad in the eighteenth century and that of Ramakrishna in the nineteenth century. He had tender-fierce visions of Kali ranging from that of a beautiful, young, pregnant woman emerging from a river and then giving birth to and suckling a child to that of a cruel, frightening hag who seized the child, stuffed it in her mouth, crushed it with her grim jaws and swallowed it, and then re-entered the river from which she had emerged.

Kali has a terrifying appearance. Her icons show a black, gaunt figure, almost naked, with a fierce face and a tongue poised to lick blood; she has gnawing teeth, sunken eyes and a garland of skulls and snakes, with weapons in her hands she dances on the body of her prostrate husband Shiva. She appears as wild, untamed, frantic and out of control. As such she is the 'mad Mother', the mistress of death, time and destruction. Her origin may well have been a fierce tribal deity who originally lacked any maternal role. But she underwent such transformation that she eventually came to be worshipped as cosmic mother with a benign, maternal character. Ramprasad celebrated Kali as the mistress of a mad, reeling world, but in spite of her demonic, frightening aspects she was for him above all the loving, compassionate Mother who invites her devotees to complete self-surrender just like a child submits to its mother. For Ramakrishna, too, Kali was the mother of a dizzy, intoxicated creation, brought forth and destroyed through Kali's wild dancing; redemption lies in the awareness that we are invited to take part in that dance. Swami Vivekananda wrote a well-known poem on 'Kali the Mother' where he says 'Terror is Thy name, Death is Thy breath', and yet he invokes her 'Come, O Mother, come' and goes on to say 'Who dares misery love, and hug the form of Death, Dance in Destruction's dance, to him the Mother comes.'

In spite of her terrifying appearance Kali is utterly benign and gracious to her devotees. It is she who bestows salvation, for she possesses the transforming and liberating power that breaks through all illusion. She destroys the finite to reveal the infinite and devotees experience bonds of close intimacy with her, often reminiscent of familial relationships, especially those between child and mother.

The Western theological imagination has been less preoccupied with locating contradictory human experiences in the Godhead, and yet the resolution of all differences and distinctions, of all paradoxes and opposites within Divine Being can be a deeply transforming and liberating insight. Calling the Divine by the name of 'Mother' whilst relating the opposites of good and bad motherly treatment to Ultimate Reality, as the Hindu tradition does, can be a more satisfying and integral experience than understanding the mother symbol as exclusively good and positive.

The Indian figure of Kali as Divine Mother is a symbol of much power and ambivalence. She has four primary aspects—as good and terrible mother, as deluder and as granter of salvation—but at the ultimate level these are all one. In her good and terrifying motherly aspects Kali is the power of the material world, especially of nature in her creative, nurturing and destructive aspects which are all interconnected. But Kali stands not only for the power of nature, but also for that of the spirit—the universe lies within her, within her womb, and all forms are transformations of her energy and vibrations of her consciousness. But this consciousness can ensnare beings in the chains of worldly desire, thus obscuring divine reality. But Kali also points the way out of illusion and delusion, for she is knowledge and love which free the devotee from all bondage. Thus Kali comes to be revealed as divine perfection and absolute freedom—she is the path to salvation.

3. The ambiguity of divine motherhood

Using motherhood as a metaphor for the Divine is inherently problematic. Difficulties arise, just as with the father image, although they are of a somewhat different nature. The idea of motherhood is often falsely idealised and only seen in the most positive terms. The following passage, in which an Indian Ramakrishna monk describes 'The Mother's Nature', implicitly points to the difficulties in linking motherhood with Ultimate Reality:

> The highest of all feminine types is the mother. Mother represents the pure love that knows no barter, no selfishness, no personal gain. The mother's is a love that never dies, and the relationship between a mother and her child the sweetest of all human relationships. If God, who is the source of all power, goodness and beauty, can be conceived of as the Divine Mother, then the best relationship we can have with her will be as her children. A child is totally dependent on its mother for everything. It is the mother's responsibility to look after it every moment of its life ... Even as the earthly mother runs to her child when it is tired ... so the Divine Mother, too, will surely reveal herself to us, once we realise the emptiness of this world and cry to her for her saving grace and protection. She will come to us and take us on her lap, if we want her and her alone. Not only will she clasp us to her bosom, but she will deliver us from the bondage of this earthly existence and transport us to a realm of peace, joy, and blessedness that passes all understanding. (Swami Ananyananda 1975, p. 10).

There are two difficulties here. No actual mother can conform to this ideal and no child depends for ever on its mother. There are many different and partial ways of experiencing motherhood and yet it is an experience in which all human beings in some way or another participate, for our mother is literally, though not exclusively, the source and beginning of our personal life. This universality of experience, shared by all human beings, makes it particularly apt for motherhood to function as a powerful symbol which evokes not only an individual's immediate family experience, but can refer to other bonds of belonging—to clan and tribe, to one's country, even to the earth and the cosmos.

But what does the symbol of motherhood connote? It points to the beginning of life, the creative source and origin. As such it is associated with primal human experiences of comfort, security, nurture, love and compassion, the security and assurance of being held, cradled, sheltered and protected. The warmth and strength of mother's freely given, unquestioning love also relates to the quality and intimacy of a relationship, to a closeness which is linked to early experiences of fusion and integration. Speaking of the Divine as 'Mother' in this sense thus expresses the richness and creativity of our original source and that of all creation; it celebrates the giving of life, the pouring out of love and compassion, the continuing ground of security and protection. Addressing, calling, imploring the Divine in motherly terms expresses our endearment, affection, closeness and even familiarity in contrast to the way where Ultimate Reality seems so remote, distant and alien.

However, the meaning of motherhood here relates to the experience of the child whose mother's womb and lap are the place of protection and refuge. Yet motherhood is not only passively experienced by the child; it is at the same time an active experience of creative involvement for women to give birth and do the mothering. In fact, it can be one of the most ecstatic and humanly rewarding experiences there is. Surely, in this active sense motherhood is one of the most powerful and resonant metaphors for divine creativity. Women in particular may feel the deep need for and experience a particular joy and confirmation in celebrating the Divine as 'Mother'— an appellation which speaks so deeply out of and to their own experience. Human motherhood can also be a fruitful source of theological insight as Margaret Hebblethwaite has shown in her study *Motherhood and God* (1984). Exploring the motherhood metaphor introduces new areas of human experience into theology which can be very illuminating and reveal hitherto unknown riches, not to forget those of spiritual motherhood.

Both the passive and active aspects of the idea of motherhood can positively strengthen and enlarge our thinking about the Divine. Yet one must not forget that motherhood can have negative aspects too and that all our attempts of speaking of the Divine as 'Mother', in spite of great gains, also point to a fundamental inadequacy of the comparison. What are in fact the limitations of the mother symbolism with regard to Divine Reality?

First of all, the mother image is not unambiguously positive. We all know the wrathful, terrifying, unreliable, moody, obsessive, and inadequate mother. This inherent ambivalence of the mother figure is well expressed in the Hindu portrayal of the mother goddess as both benevolent and terrifying, though ultimately the positive elements overcome the negative ones. Christian theologians would do well to reflect on the rich resources and multiple meanings of divine motherhood in Hinduism where so many different facets come so beautifully together.

A second limitation relates to women's own experience and identity. The idea of a Divine Mother, however inspiring and confirming, is not entirely helpful as it exalts motherhood to the exclusion of all else and thus severely circumscribes the range of woman's life and aspirations. It equates femaleness with giving birth and leaves little room for an identity or independence of women apart from being mothers. Historically speaking, it is surprising that the new emphasis on linking motherhood and the Divine in a new way in Christian thought comes at a time when women's lives are actually much less involved with being mothers than at any previous time in history.

The third difficulty is perhaps the greatest of all, for it concerns the problematic of using parental images for divine-human relationships. Such images emphasise the childlike nature of human beings. Yet it is a natural part of human growth for the child to gain full confidence and step into life out on its own. The child has to seek separation from the mother to find independence and integration at a new level. We all dread onesided dependence and yearn for adult relationships of true equality and mutual interdependence in reassuring love and trust.

Here the mother image of the Divine may be just as enslaving as the father image, an image of parental authority, hierarchical relationships, and even greater dependence. Psychologically speaking it makes good sense to think that human beings initially develop their God image in analogy to that of their preferred parent, but just as eventually we need to relate to our parents as people in their own right rather than as authority figures on whom we remain dependent, so also our image of Divine Reality must grow to new and larger dimensions which far transcend the associations of early childhood. What we need perhaps most of all to find human maturity and wholeness is a separation from a mythological God image, far too narrowly circumscribed and imprisoned by the image of either motherhood or fatherhood. But given the continuing need for using meaningful images for Divine Being, Presence and Power, it seems clear that once the limitations are acknowledged, contemporary Christians can be greatly enriched by using the name of 'Mother' as well as 'Father' in devotion, prayer and liturgical celebration. Similarly, theological reflection will be enlarged and deepened by the further exploration of divine motherhood symbolism whilst women will feel that a very central part of their experience is validated and affirmed in a new way by linking motherhood to the Divine itself.

References

M. Hebblethwaite, *Motherhood and God* (London 1984).

D. R. Kinsley, *The Sword and the Flute* (Berkeley 1975); *idem., Hindu Goddesses. Visions of the Divine in the Hindu Religious Tradition* (Berkeley 1986).

A. E. Lewis, ed., *The Motherhood of God.* A Report by a Study Group appointed by the Women's Guild and the Panel on Doctrine on the invitation of the General Assembly of the Church of Scotland (Edinburgh 1984).

C. MacKenzie Brown, 'Kālī, the Mad Mother', in C. Olson, ed., *The Book of the Goddess* (New York 1983), pp. 110–23.

W. Madtha, 'Sakti: The Feminine Aspect of God in Indian Tradition', in *Journal of Dharma*: Feminine Aspect of God, V/2 (1980), pp. 175–89.

Swami Ananyananda, 'God as the Divine Mother', in *Vedanta for East and West* 143 (1975), pp. 2–10.

Sallie McFague

Mother God[1]

WE CAN speak of God only indirectly, using our world and ourselves as metaphors for expressing our relationship with the divine. One of the oldest and most powerful metaphors has been the parental one; however, in the Christian tradition only one parent—the father—has been allowed to image God. To be sure, maternal language is very prevalent in other ways: for the Church, in relation to Mary, as the proper role for all women. But as a metaphor for relating to God, Christians have been wary.

One must ask why this is the case. Surely one reason is Christianity's Hebraic heritage in which Yahweh, the one, holy, transcendent deity defeats the fertility goddesses of early Mediterranean culture. This tradition does not easily accommodate the female (as it does not accommodate nature or the body either). The male sky God under whom all things are hierarchically and dualistically ordered became the pattern for subsequent theology, as it also became the pattern for much of Western culture. The hierarchical dualisms which are so prevalent in our ways of thinking owe much to the patriarchal understanding of the divine: God as the dominating head of the family of 'man' became a form of social organisation which supported other hierarchical dualisms such as male/female, spirit/flesh, human beings/nature, white people/people of colour, rich/poor, straight/ gay, Christian/non-Christian. Patriarchal language for God promotes an entire way of thinking, social constructions of race, class, and gender, for instance, that benefit males, especially white, affluent males.

In this essay, we will experiment with the metaphor or model of God as mother in order to decentre the patriarchal model and to provide an alternative to it. It will also serve to recontextualise the paternal model in a

138

parental direction, in opposition to its traditional patriarchal direction (having been assimilated into the monarchical, triumphalistic language of God as king, master, and lord). As we begin this experiment, we must avoid several possible pitfalls. First, the intention is not to turn the tables and establish a new hierarchical dualism with a matriarchal model of God. Rather, it is to investigate a rich—and neglected, if not repressed and suppressed—source for expressing some aspects of the God/world relationship in our time, most specifically, the interdependence and mutuality of all life. In our contemporary world which is increasingly a global village and in which ecological deterioration and nuclear holocaust are definite possibilities, we need to underscore the interconnectedness of all living things. A model of God as mother of the earth and all its beings is a strong candidate for encouraging a sensibility that will support the realities of late twentieth century existence.

Second, we must not sentimentalise maternal imagery. We will not suppose that mothers are 'naturally' loving, comforting, or self-sacrificing. Our society has a stake in making women think that they are biologically-programmed to be these things, when, in fact, a good case can be made that the so-called qualities or stereotypes of mothers are social constructions—women are not born, but become, mothers through education and imitation.[2] Rather, we will focus on the most basic things that females (as mothers) do among most, if not all the species and which human mothers do as well: give birth, feed and protect the young, want the young to flourish.

Third, we need to recognise how dangerous and oppressive maternal language can be, both to women and to all human beings in relation to God. It poses problems for women because it suggests that women who are not mothers are not true or fulfilled women; it gives power to the one role that has probably oppressed women more than any other over the centuries; it can appear to be pro-life or anti-abortion at a time when population problems loom very large on the horizon. Therefore, we must be careful to see this model of God as only *one* model and by no means one that would eliminate speaking of God as sister, as midwife, or in other female terms. The model poses problems for all human beings in relation to God because if the parental model, mother or father, is used exclusively for God, it places us always in the role of children. At a time when we need desperately to be 'adults', to take responsibility for our world and its well-being, we cannot support a model that suggests that the 'great mother' or 'great father' will take care of our crises of poverty, discrimination, damage to the ecosystem, and so forth.

Nevertheless, in spite of all these qualifications, the maternal metaphor is so powerful and so right for our time that we *should* use it. If the heart of Christian faith for an ecological, nuclear-threatened age must be a profound awareness of the preciousness and vulnerability of life as a gift we receive and pass on, with appreciation for its value and desire for its fulfilment, it is difficult to think of any metaphor more apt than the parental one and especially the maternal one. God as the giver of life, as the power of being in all being, can be imaged through the metaphor of mother—and of father. Parental love is the most powerful and intimate experience we have of giving love whose return is not calculated (though a return is appreciated): it is the gift of *life as such* to others. Parental love wills life and when it comes, exclaims, 'It is good that you exist!'[3] Moreover, in addition to being the gift of life, parental love nurtures what it has brought into existence, and wants it to grow and be fulfilled. These are the three basic features of the model which we will investigate.

The physical act of giving birth is the base from which this model derives its power, for here it joins the reservoir of the great symbols of life and of life's continuity: blood, water, breath, sex, and food. In the acts of conception, gestation, and birth all are involved, and it is therefore no surprise that these symbols became the centre of most religions, including Christianity, for they have the power to express the renewal and transformation of life—the 'second birth'—because they are the basis of our 'first birth'. And yet, at least in Christianity, our first birth has been strangely neglected; another way of saying this is that creation, the birth of the universe and all its beings, has not been permitted the imagery that this tradition uses so freely for redemption, the transformation and fulfilment of creation. Why is this the case?

One reason is surely that Christianity, alienated as it always has been for female sexuality, has been willing to image the second, 'spiritual', renewal of existence in the birth metaphor, but not the first, 'physical', coming into existence. In the Judaeo-Christian tradition, creation has been imaginatively pictured as an intellectual, aesthetic 'act' of God, accomplished through God's word and wrought by God's 'hands', much as a painting is created by an artist or a form by a sculptor. But the model of God as mother suggests a very different kind of creation, one which underscores the radical dependence of all things on God, but in an internal rather than an external fashion. Thus, if we wish to understand the world as in some fashion 'in' God rather than God as 'in' the world, it is clearly the parent *as mother* that is the stronger candidate for an understanding of creation as bodied forth from the divine being. For it is the imagery of gestation, giving birth, and lactation that creates an imaginative picture of creation that is profoundly dependent on and cared for by divine life.[4] There is simply no other imagery available to us that has this power for expressing the interdependence and inter-relatedness of all life with its ground. All of us, female and male, have the womb as our first home, all of us are born from the bodies of our mothers, most of us are fed by our mothers. What better imagery could there be for expressing the most basic reality of existence: that we—all of us in our planet and the entire rest of the universe—live and move and have our being in God.

Of equal importance to the birth aspect is the ability of the model to express the nurturing of life. Parents feed the young. This is, across the entire range of life, the most basic responsibility of parents, often of fathers as well as mothers. Among most animals, it is instinctual and often accomplished only at the cost of the health or life of the parent. It is not principally from altruistic motives that parents feed the young but from a base close to the one that brought new life into existence, the source that participates in passing life along. With human parents, the same love that says, 'It is good that you exist!' desires that life to continue, and for many parents in much of the world that is a daily and often horrendous struggle. There is, perhaps, no picture more powerful to express 'giving' love than that of parents wanting, but not having the food, to feed their children.

The Christian tradition has paid a lot of attention to food imagery, in fact, one could say it is central to it: from Jesus feeding the crowds and eating with sinners to the eucharistic meal as the main sacrament of the Church. But, again, as with the birth imagery, it has spiritualised the imagery, and has not taken with utmost seriousness the physical necessity of food. One of the implications of adopting the maternal model would be the restoration of food as a necessity for all of God's children. A theology that sees God as the parent who feeds the young and by extension, the weak and the vulnerable, understands God as caring about the most basic needs of life in its struggle to continue. A justice ethic is the direct implication of the maternal model: *all* the children must be fed.

Finally, God as mother (parent) wants *all* to flourish.[5] God is the mother of all existence, all beings, as well as the ecosystem that supports them, and while human parents tend to focus on our own species and specific individuals within that species, God as mother is impartial and inclusive as we can never be. The fulfilment of the entire created order, its growth and well-being, is the wish of the mother who brought it into being and who nurtures it. Again we see the implications for how we view the world: our anthropocentric bias which understands all other creatures and things in the world as instruments for our use is undercut. If we take a 'theocentric' point of view, we also must take a 'cosmocentric' point of view, for the mother/creator of all that is loves *all*, not just human beings. We see here also the relationship of the mother and judge models: God the mother judges those who thwart the nurture and fulfilment of her beloved creation. God as mother is angry because some of her created beings desire everything for themselves, not recognising the *intrinsic* worth of other beings. In this view, 'sin' is not 'against God', the pride and rebellion of an inferior against a superior, but 'against the body', the refusal to be part of an ecological whole whose continued existence and success depends upon a recognition of the interdependence and interrelatedness of all species. The mother-God as creator, then, is also involved in 'economics', the management of the household of the universe, to ensure the just distribution of goods to *all*.

What is also evident is that this model undercuts the hierarchical dualism of the tradition and of the Genesis creation story in which God, absolutely distinct from and external to the world, creates it, with a hierarchy of beings. An alternative imaginative picture emerges from the model of God as mother. The kind of creation that fits with this model is creation not as an intellectual or artistic act but as a physical event: the universe is bodied forth from God, it is expressive of God's very being: it could, therefore, be seen as God's 'body'.[6] It is not something alien to God but is from the 'womb' of God, formed through 'gestation', a process symbolising the long evolutionary history of the universe. There are important implications of our picture, but first we must remind ourselves that it is a picture—but so is the artistic, intellectual model of creation. We are not claiming that God creates by giving birth to the universe as her body; what we are suggesting is that the birth metaphor is both closer to Christian faith and to a contemporary, evolutionary, ecological context than the alternative craftsman model.

A critical implication of our model is that it overturns the dualisms of mind and body, spirit and flesh, humanity and nature, male and female. God's body, that which supports all life, is not matter or spirit but the matrix out of which everything evolves. In this picture, God is not spirit over against a world of matter, with human beings dangling in between, chained to their bodies but eager to escape to the world of spirit. The universe, from God's being, is properly body (as well as spirit) because in some sense God is physical (as well as beyond the physical). This shocking idea—that God is physical—is one of the most important implications of the model of creation by God the mother. It is an explicit rejection of Christianity's long, oppressive, and dangerous alliance with spirit against body, an alliance that has oppressed women as well as nature and for the good of all needs to come to an end.

In closing this experiment with the model of God as mother, I would stress that it is an 'experiment'. It is an heuristic, imaginative enterprise. As a remythologisation, such theology acknowledges that it is, as it were, painting a picture. For most people, the imaginative picture of the relationship between God and the world they hold influences their behaviour more powerfully than concepts do. In a time when life on our planet is threatened in so many ways, an imaginative picture that underscores the radical and intimate interrelatedness and interdependence of all life; that insists that the basic necessities of life must be justly shared; that insists that species other than human being have intrinsic worth; and that undercuts dualistic hierarchies of all sorts is the sort of picture needed. No imaginative picture of the God of Christianity—the God who is on the side of life and its fulfilment—can last forever, because what is understood as 'fulfilment', as salvation, changes. We must try out new pictures that will bring the reality of God's love into the imaginations of the women and men of today just as others have done in Scripture and the tradition. God as mother is *one* powerful model appropriate for our time; it is by no means the only one.

Notes

1. This essay is based in part on my book, *Models of God: Theology for an Ecological, Nuclear Age* (Philadelphia 1987).
2. See Nancy Chodorow, *The Reproduction of Mothering: Psychoanalysis and the Sociology of Gender* (Berkeley 1978).
3. The phrase is from Josef Pieper, *About Love*, trans. Richard and Clara Winston (Chicago 1974), p. 22.
4. Paul Tillich says that the symbolic dimension of the 'ground of being' points to the mother-quality of giving birth, carrying, and embracing' (*Systematic Theology*, Chicago 1963, Vol. 3, pp. 293–294). Arthur Peacocke sees maternal, creation imagery as a corrective to the traditional view: '... it is an analogy of God creating the world within herself ... God creates a world that is, in principle and in origin, other than him/herself but creates it ... within him/herself' (*Creation and the World of Science*, Oxford 1979, p. 142).
5. This must not be interpreted as a pro-life or anti-abortion stance. If the various species are to thrive, not every individual in every species can be fulfilled. In a closed ecological system with limits on natural resources, difficult decisions must be made to ensure the continuation, growth, and fulfilment of the many forms of life (not just one form and not all of its individuals).
6. This image, radical as it may seem, is an old one with roots in Stoicism and elliptically in the Hebrew Scriptures. For a treatment of its Christian history and contemporary viability, as well as a critique of creation *ex nihilo*, see Grace Jantzen, *God's World, God's Body* (Philadelphia/London 1984).

Gregory Baum

Bulletin: The Apostolic Letter *Mulieris dignitatem*

POPE JOHN Paul II has decided to give his Apostolic Letter, *Mulieris dignitatem*, on the theology of women, the style and character of a meditation. The Letter, dated 15 August 1988, is in fact a meditation on Scripture and the experience of the Church. The Letter is not so much an authoritative expression of the magisterium as a papal response to an ongoing conversation in the Church.

There are several ways of reading an ecclesiastical text. It is possible to compare the text with the Church's antecedant teaching and thus focus on the *novum* of the text. Such a reading brings out the doctrinal development taking place in the ecclesiastical magisterium. A close look at the evolution of the Church's official teaching reveals that the Vatican not only teaches the Church but also learns from the Church. Robert Dionne's recent book, *The Papacy and the Church*[1], offers a detailed study of the changing positions of the Roman magisterium on seven topics from the pontificate of Pius IX (1846) to the Second Vatican Council, including the teaching on the separation of Church and state, religious liberty as a human right, the truth contained in non-Christian religions, the identification of the Catholic Church with Christ's Mystical Body, and the Church's relation to non-Catholic Christians. Dionne demonstrates that in these instances the Popes have in fact learnt from the Church.

Yet it also possible to read an ecclesiastical text in order to understand its total meaning and relate this meaning to the ongoing theological debate in the Church.

In this brief article I wish to present these two readings of *Mulieris dignitatem.*

1. The 'novum' in the Letter

Pope John Paul II uses a hermeneutical approach in reading the biblical texts that leads him to interpretations that differ strikingly from the interpretations given by the Church Fathers and the Church's traditional teaching. The Pope begins by discerning 'the signs of the times' and then reads Scripture to discover what it has to say in regard to these signs. This is the approach adopted by the Pope in some of his encyclicals.

In the Letter, *Mulieris dignitatem,* the relevant sign of the times is the increasing attention given to the dignity and vocation of women. The Pope recalls that John XXIII had designated a sign of the times the fact that 'women are becoming ever more conscious of their human dignity, that they will no longer tolerate being treated as inanimate objects or mere instruments, that they claim rather, in domestic and in public life, the rights and duties that befit a human person.'[2] This sign of the times, acknowledged in Vatican II's *Gaudium et spes,*[3] is reconfirmed in the present Letter.

What does the Bible have to say in regard to this sign of the times? According to the Letter, the Scriptures confirm the equality between men and women. In Genesis we read that men and women were created in God's image. Men and women are equally images of God. That is why Scripture ascribes to God masculine and feminine characteristics. God is father and mother. This anthropomorphic language must be understood in a truly theological way. While there is a certain similarity between God and creatures, the dissimilarity is always greater. Thus God's generative power is neither masculine nor feminine; it is totally divine. God is spirit. God's fatherhood is free of all masculinity, it is not patriarchal, it is ultracorporal, superhuman, completely divine.[4]

According to Genesis, the Letter argues, God created the first couple in perfect equality. Men and women have different characteristics, but they were created equal. Their relationship was not patriarchal. We read that Eve, made from Adam's body, was meant to be his helper and that therefore women are dependent on men and destined to serve them. Yet according to the Letter, men are also dependent on women and destined to serve women.[5] God created men and women in equality, free of subordination, in perfect mutuality. This, the Letter argues, is the eternal truth.

Patriarchy is brought about by human sin and divine punishment. In the fall, men and women lose their equality.[6] Humankind becomes deeply divided. Men are now appointed as rulers over women. Yet this patriarchal subjugation of women is accompanied by the promise of redemption. Throughout the history of Israel, the prophets longed for this redemption, for the return of God's original plan, beyond patriarchy, of equality, co-responsibility and love.

This new order, the Letter argues, was brought by Jesus. While in the Old Testament, God in covenanting the people addressed only men, in the New Testament God's word inaugurating redemption is addressed to Mary, a woman.[7] According to the Letter, Jesus promoted the true dignity of women. His words and his actions did not reflect the discrimination prevalent in his culture. He even appointed the woman at the well (John 4) disciple and evangelist, 'an event without precedent'.[8] Women were the first witnesses of the resurrection and the first to announce the truth to the apostles. With Rabanus Maurus and Thomas Aquinas the Letter calls Mary Magdalen 'the apostle of the apostles'. Here, in the new order, womanhood receives 'an new dimension'.[9]

It is in the light of this new dimension that the Letter reads the Pauline epistles. The promise of redemption includes the equality of men and women. In Christ all discrimination disappears. Even the passages where the epistles speak of the subordination of women must be interpreted in the light of the new dimension. It is written that women are to be subject to their husbands, but the new dimension makes us understand that husbands must also be subject to their wives.[10] While husband and wife have different roles and different characteristics, they are equals, they enjoy perfect mutuality. When Paul says that the woman is obedient to her spouse as the Church is to Jesus Christ, we must understand the difference between the two relations. The husband is also obedient to his wife and hence the mutuality between the sexes is preserved, while Christ is the head of the Church and in no sense obedient to her.[11]

According to the Letter, the divine revelation recorded in Scripture transcends the culture in which it was composed. God is not patriarchal, neither is the relation between men and women as defined by God's creation and redemption. This is the eternal truth about God and humans. The Letter adds that just as slavery, rejected by divine revelation in principle, was overcome only gradually in the course of history, so it was with the subjugation of women.[12] Their subjugation is being overcome at this time.

2. Potential for motherhood

John Paul II has his own, original way of reading the Bible. His understanding of the transhistorical nature of divine revelation is unusual. And the unreflected ease with which the Letter contrasts the superior ethios of Jesus with the ethical ideals of the rabbis is also problematic. Still, following his method, the Pope offers a reading of biblical texts that transcends traditional interpretations. At the same time, the Letter does not conclude that 'the new dimension' brought by Christ, the overcoming of women's subordination, demands that the equality of men and women, lost through the sin of Adam, must be given visible, institutional, sacramental expression in the worshiping community which is the Church. The Letter does not conclude that the ordination of women would make the Church a more authentic sign and symbol of God's coming reign. Why not?

Men and woman are equal, yet they are also different. The Letter argues that masculinity and feminity have been given distinct characteristics by the Creator. This distinction is also eternal. To clarify the essence of feminity the Letter mediates on the Blessed Virgin Mary, Mother of Jesus, Mother of God, destined to play a critical role in the advent of Christ and Christ's redemption. Principally the essence of womanhood is motherhood or potential for motherhood.[13] The woman receives the gift, gives birth to the child, and becomes forever carer and nurturer. For some women this potential for motherhood is lived out spiritually in the state of virginity: here the gift is the Word of God received in faith and birthing, caring and nurturing acquire spiritual meaning.

In their struggle for their human rights, the Letter argues, women must not become masculine: they must not appropriate to themselves characteristics contrary to their original feminity.[14] The Letter does not clarify what this means. Does this mean, for instance, the women should not assume positions of leadership in public life? The Letter is silent here. While John XXIII regarded the active presence of women in public life as part of the sign of the times, the Letter does not pursue this line of thought. Indeed, if the Blessed Virgin Mary sums up the vocation of womanhood then participation in society as thinkers, inventors, initiators, presiders and leaders is hardly part of the divinely appointed destiny of women. Such a position would be wholly unacceptable to contemporary men and women.

When the Letter deals with the ordination of women, it appeals to the fact that Jesus called only men to become apostles. The Letter might have interpreted this event in the light of what it had called 'the new dimension' and argued that to limit the ordained ministry to men alone would assign the priesthood to the old order, rather than the new. But this line of thought is not pursued. The Letter knows that 'in calling only men as his apostles, Christ acted in a completely free and sovereign manner, not in conformity with the customs of his time'.[15] What is refuted here is the argument that Jesus simply followed the practice of his own culture. Jesus chose to exclude women from the ordained ministry because the priest, acting *in persona Christi*, represents Christ and thus embodies masculine, not feminine characteristics. This surely does not mean that male genitals are a requirement for priesthood. What the Letter intends, one must suppose, is that priesthood demands spiritual masculine characteristics, the ability to exercise leadership in the realm of the spirit. Potential motherhood which is the genius of women makes them unfit for ordination.

One of the weaknesses of the Letter is that it does not spell out but only hints at the difference between male and female characteristics. The difference, we are told, does not introduce inequality between men and women, it does not interrupt mutuality, it does not constitute hierarchical subordination. But if that is true, one may not identify masculinity with vocation for leadership and feminity with its absence. The Letter is not coherent at this point.

There are, however, redeeming inconsistencies in the Letter that deserve to be mentioned. When discussing the exclamation of the woman, 'Blessed is the womb that bore you and the breasts that you sucked' (Luke 11:27), and the answer of Jesus, 'Blessed rather are those who hear the word of God and keep it', the Letter recognises the genius of feminity in every believer, male or female.[16] And when discussing the Pauline theme of the Church as Bride of Christ, the Letter recognises that every believer, male and female, has a bridal relationship to Christ and hence participates in femininity.[17] At the present time, the Letter argues, when the world is becoming more deeply divided between the powerful and the powerless and when human suffering is acquiring massive proportions, we 'impatiently await the manifestation of that "genius" which belongs to women and which ensures sensitivity for human beings in every circumstance—because they are human and because "the greatest of these is love" (1 Cor. 13:13).'[18] But if feminity is understood as universal compassion then Jesus himself becomes the earthly embodiment of the feminine principle. The Letter does not escape the contradictions of every discourse that defines the spiritual characteristics of masculinity and feminity. Since masculine and feminine characteristics are found in all people, in men and in women, it does not seem logical to refer to these characteristics as 'masculine' or 'feminine'. Virtue has no gender. Faith, hope and love have no gender. Intelligence has many manifestations, but they cannot be classified as masculine or feminine.

If we understand *Mulieris dignitatem* as an attempt of the Pope to enter into conversation with the entire Church, then we admire the clear recognition on the part of the magisterium that God is father and mother, that generativity has no gender, and that according to God's creation the man-woman relation is not patriarchal. Yet in my opinion, missing in the Letter is a longer reflection on the sign of the times, *i.e.* the presence of women in *public life*. Today women no longer define themselves through their potential for motherhood. Women continue to be good mothers, but they include in their self-definition the full human vocation, including their role as thinkers, actors, and leaders. Does one want to read the Bible as if it urged modern women to withdraw from public life? It may be sounder to emphasise the multiplicity of charisms and vocations in Church and society, which God distributes among women and men in a manner that continues to surprise us.

Notes

1. Robert Dionne, *The Papacy and the Church* (New York 1987).
2. *Pacem in terris*, n. 41.
3. *Gaudium et spes*, n. 9.
4. *Mulieris dignitatem*, n. 6.
5. *Ibid.*, n. 5.
6. *Ibid.*, n. 10.
7. *Ibid.*, n. 11.
8. *Ibid.*, n. 15.
9. *Ibid.*, n. 16.
10. *Ibid.*, n. 24.
11. *Ibid.*.
12. *Ibid.*.
13. *Ibid.*, n. 18.
14. *Ibid.*, n. 10.
15. *Ibid.*, n. 26.
16. *Ibid.*, n. 19.
17. *Ibid.*, n. 25.
18. *Ibid.*, n. 30.

Contributors

GREGORY BAUM was born in Berlin in 1923 and has been resident in Canada since 1940. He was a student at McMaster University, Hamilton, Canada; Ohio State University, USA; the University of Fribourg, Switzerland; and the New School for Social Research, New York. He is now professor of theology and social ethics at McGill University, Montreal. He is editor of the *Ecumenist*. His publications include: *Religion and Alienation* (1975), *The Social Imperative* (1978), *Catholics and Canadian Socialism* (1980), *The Priority of Labor* (1982), *Ethics and Economics* (1984), *Theology and Society* (1987).

DORRY DE BEIJER was born in 1956 in Rotterdam, The Netherlands. She studied theology at Nijmegen University and has been the study secretary of the action group 'Vrouw en Kerk van de Katholieke Raad voor Kerk en Samenleving' since 1987. She is co-author of *Op Water en Brood: Vrouwen vieren Liturgie* (Baarn 1981) and has published various articles on the subject of women studies/theology. She has also written two articles about a feminist view of the new reproductive technology in *Lover* (literary review for the women's movement) 1987 (2) and in *Mara* (journal for feminism and theology) 1989 (2).

MARIE-THÉRÈSE VAN LUNEN CHENU is a Frenchwoman. She was born in 1931, married a Dutchman and lived until 1980 in Brussels with their five children. She was one of the founders of the international group 'Men and Women in the Church' and took an active part in the drafting of their Bulletin and the establishment of the Women and Christianity Research and Documentation Centre in the Catholic Faculty at Lyon. She has written numerous articles on feminist questions and particularly on

CONTRIBUTORS 151

their interaction in society and the Church, including those on 'Women, Feminism and Theology' in *Initiation à la pratique de la théologie*, Vol. 5, (1987), and 'Living in the Family?' in *Visages de la Famille* (1975).

MARY CONDREN was born in Dublin, Ireland, and is a writer and teacher on theology and feminist theory. She has been editor of *Movement*, a journal of theology and politics of the Student Christian Movement, and is former co-ordinator of the European Women's Project of the World Student Christian Federation. She has studied at the University of Hull, England, Boston College, and Harvard University, and has been a Research Resource Associate in Women's Studies at Harvard Divinity School. She has written many articles on women and theology, and *The Serpent and the Goddess: Women, Religion and Power in Celtic Ireland* (San Francisco 1989).

IVONE GEBARA, a Sister of the Congregation of Our Lady, lectures in philosophy and theology at the Theological Institute of Recife in Brazil. She is a member of DEPA, an inter-disciplinary organisation for training pastoral agents to work among the people. She has published articles on the Church and the poor, the place of women in the Church and popular education, in leading journals in Brazil, and is co-author, with Maria Clara Bingemer, of *Mary: Mother of God, Mother of the Poor* in the series 'Liberation and Theology' (1989).

CHRISTINE GUDORF is professor of ethics in the Theology Department of Xavier University, Cincinnati, Ohio. Her PhD is from Columbia University in a joint programme with Union Theological Seminary. She is Roman Catholic, married, the mother of three sons, and has published articles and edited books on feminist ethics, case method ethics, liberation theology, and sexual ethics. Her dissertation was published as *Catholic Social Teaching on Liberation Themes* (Washington, DC 1980).

CATHARINA HALKES (born 1920) is emeritus professor of feminism and Christianity at the Catholic University of Nijmegen. She is one of the founders of the feminist theological journal *Mara* and one of the editors of the series 'Examples of women's studies in theology'. Her publications, most of which have appeared in German translation, include *Storm na de stilte: de plaats van de vrouw in de kerk* (Utrecht 1964); *De horizon van het pastorale gesprek* (Haarlem 1977); (edited with Daan Buddingh) *Als vrouwen aan het woord komen* (Kampen 1977); *Met Mirjam is het begonnen: opstandige vrouwen op zoek naar hun geloof* (Kampen 1980); *Op water en brood; vrouwen vieren liturgie* (Baarn 1981); *Zoekend naar wat verloren ging: enkele aanzetten voor een feministische theologie* (Baarn 1984); *Feminisme en Spiritualiteit* (Baarn 1986); . . . *En alles zal worden herschapen: gedachten over de heelwording van de schepping in het spanningsveld tussen natuur en cultuur* (Baarn 1989). She has also contributed numerous articles to theological and other periodicals and to symposia.

URSULA KING (née Brenke) STL (Paris), MA (Delhi), PhD (London), studied theology, philosophy and comparative religion in Germany, France, India and England. She has written the entry on 'Feminismus' in *Evangelisches Kirchenlexikon* (vol. I, Göttingen 1986), edited a book on *Women in the World's Religions, Past and Present* (New York 1987) and published *Women and Spirituality. Voices of Protest and Promise* (London and New York 1989) and *The Spirit of One Earth. Reflections on Teilhard de Chardin and Global Spirituality* (New York 1989).

JOHANNA KOHN-ROELIN was born in Vienna in 1960. She studied Catholic theology in Munster and Frankfurt. From 1986–8 she taught at the Teacher Training Institute of the Catholic Faculty in Munster. She is a member of the youth committee of the International Council of Christians and Jews and since May 1989 a member of the directorate of the German Co-ordinating Council of Jewish-Christian Societies in West Germany. At present she is working on a dissertation on history and guilt as a task for feminist theology in theology after Auschwitz. She is married with one daughter. Her publications include: *Hashoah. Christliche-jüdische Verständigung nach Auschwitz* (Mainz/Munich 1986); with J. B. Metz, 'Auschwitz' in U. Ruh, D. Seeber and R. Walter, *Handwörterbuch religiöser Gegenwartsfragen* (Freiburg/Basel/Vienna 1986), pp. 34–38; 'Christlicher Feminismus nach Auzschwitz. Aspekte einer geschichtlichen Selbstverge-wisserung' in Christine Schaumberge (ed.), *Anfrage 1. Diskussionen Feministischer Theologie. Weil wir nich vergessen wollen . . . zu einer Feministischen Theologie im Deutschen Kontext* (Munster 1987), pp. 47–58.

SALLIE McFAGUE is Carpenter Professor of Theology at Vanderbilt University and has written extensively on religious language. Her most recent book, *Models of God: Theology for an Ecological, Nuclear Age* (Philadelphia 1987) won an award for Excellence from the American Academy of Religion.

ELS MAECKELBERGHE was born in Ostend, Belgium in 1961. She studied theology and the sciences of religion at the Catholic University of

Louvain. Since 1986, she has been employed in the faculty of theology of the University of Groningen in the Netherlands and since 1989 in the service of the NWO. She has published a number of articles on Mary and is at present preparing a dissertation in which she analyses and evaluates feminist re-interpretations of Mary.

MERCY AMBA ODUYOYE is a Ghanaian Methodist, with theological education from the University of Ghana and Cambridge University. She is married to Modupe Oduyoye. Her working life has been divided between ecumenical youth work and high school teaching in Christian studies. She was a senior lecturer in the Department of Religious Studies, University of Ibadan, Nigeria (1974–86), and during that period was editor of the department's journal *Orita*. Her articles on Christianity in Africa appear in ecumenical publications and scholarly journals in Africa. She is the author of the Orbis book *Hearing and Knowing*, a theological reflection on Christianity in Africa. She has been guest lecturer in seminaries in Africa and the USA and continues to research and write on African Christianity, Christian theology and issues of feminism in Africa. She is now working in Geneva with the World Council of Churches as deputy general secretary and staff moderator of the Programme Unit on Education and Renewal.

URSULA PFÄFFLIN was born in 1943 and has two children. She studied theology and trained as a pastoral psychologist. She was pastor in Hamburg-Wilhelmsburg (1970–81), lecturer in practical theology, University of Kiel (1981–) and assistant professor of pastoral care and counselling, Bethany Theological Seminary, Chicago (1987–8). Since 1988 she has been assistant professor of pastoral care and counselling in the Christian Theological Seminary of Indianapolis. Her publications include: (ed., with Ursula Pfäfflin), *Neue Mütterlichkeit* (Gütersloh 1986), 'Pastoral-psychologisiche Aspekte feministischer Seelsorge und Beratung' in *Wege zum Menschen* 39 (May/June 1987) 226–235, 'Psychologie und Spiritualität' in Maria Kassel (ed.), *Feministische Theologie* (Stuttgart 1988).

JANE SCHABERG is professor of Religious Studies at the University of Detroit. She received her PhD at Union Theological Seminary, New York, and is the author of *The Father, the Son and the Holy Spirit: The triadic phrase in Matt. 28:19* (Chico 1982); *The illegitimacy of Jesus: A Feminist Theological Interpretation of the New Testament Infancy Narratives* (San Francisco 1987); and of articles in *New Testament Studies*; *Journal for the Study of Judaism*; *International Christian Digest*; and the J. Louis Martyn Festschrift, *Apocalyptic and the New Testament*, ed. M. J. Soards (Sheffield

1988). Her work has been deeply influenced by an awareness of the conditions of poverty, discrimination and danger in which many live in downtown Detroit.

MARIE-THERES WACKER was born in the Lower Rhine area in 1952. She is married with two daughters. She studied theology at Bonn, Tübingen and Jerusalem. Dr. Theol. (1981). From 1981 to mid-1989 an assistant at the University of Paderborn, she is presently not in paid employment. Her planned post-doctoral lecturing qualification is on the prophet Hosea. Since 1983 she has undertaken work with a feminist-theological approach, and is a member of the European Society of Women for Theological Research. Her publications include: *Weltordnung und Gericht* (Würzburg [2]1985); *Der Gott der Männer und die Frauen* (ed.) (Düsseldorf 1987) (Italian translation in preparation); *Theologie—feministisch. Disziplinen—Schwerpunkte—Richtungen* (ed.) (Düsseldorf 1988); 'Matriarchale Bibelkritik—ein antijudaistisches Konzept?' in Leonore Siegele-Wenschkewitz (ed.), *Verdrängte Vergangenheit, die uns bedrängt* (Munich 1988), pp. 181–242.

CONCILIUM

CONCILIUM

CONCILIUM 1988

All back issues are still in print: available from bookshops or direct from the publishers (£5.95/US$11.95/Can$12.75 excluding postage and packing).

T & T CLARK LTD, 59 GEORGE STREET EDINBURGH EH2 2LQ, SCOTLAND

International Theological Conference

On the occasion of the 25th anniversary
of CONCILIUM

from September 9–14, 1990, at the University of Leuven

THEME: ON THE THRESHOLD OF THE THIRD MILLENIUM

THE THEME of the conference is in three sections. The first will review the recent past of church and world and evaluate both positive and negative aspects.
Speakers: E. Schüssler Fiorenza and C. Duquoc

A more analytical and descriptive second section deals with the choice for life or death.
Speakers: J. Moltmann and D. Tracy

The third section especially involves the religious and theological manner of speaking about God and the coming kingdom of God as salvation and well-being of and for mankind.
Speakers: H. Küng and G. Gutiérrez

The lectures will be printed in advance in February 1990 in a special conference issue of CONCILIUM. This will allow emphasis during the actual conference to fall on group discussion and plenary meetings.

With this announcement CONCILIUM invites all those interested in the conference to take part in it as observers.

We would welcome your applications addressed to the General Secretariat of CONCILIUM, c/o Mrs. E. Duindam-Deckers, Prins Bernardstraat 2, 6521 AB Nijmegen, The Netherlands.

We can also supply information about inexpensive lodgings.

The registration fee for the conference is US $15.00

We would like to request that all Faculties and Institutes pin up a notice about this conference in a place appropriate to informing any interested visitors about it. For this you can use a copy (enlarged) of the Announcement.

INTERNATIONAL
CONGRESS
FOR THEOLOGY

ON THE THRESHOLD OF THE THIRD MILLENNIUM

TUESDAY EVENING, SEPTEMBER 11, 1990

Panel Discussion: Present Situation of Theology in the World

Theologians from different continents and cultures will report on the present situation of theology in the Church in their countries.

The introductions will be followed by a general discussion to give members and observers a chance to exchange their opinions in a plenary session.